D1709573

The
HOMEMADE
PIZZA
COOKBOOK BIBLE

[2 in 1] Step-by-Step Guide to Make a Perfect Pizza with 1000 Days of Authentic Recipes: From Italian Tradition to Irresistible American Style Classics

ANTONY DE LUCA

Welcome, Dear Reader!

Thank you for choosing my book. Whether you are a beginner or seeking fresh challenges and inspiration, I am confident you will find pages to your liking within the book :)

I've also recorded a video for you, right in my kitchen, **guiding you step by step** on achieving a truly authentic Neapolitan pizza because **learning by watching** is often easier than reading.

Towards the end, you'll find the link to the **FULL VIDEO TUTORIAL**

Let's create together irresistible pizzas!

Antony De Luca

Table of Contents

Pizza: Raise your hand if you don't love pizza!

We're so infatuated with this dish that there isn't a region in the world where the word "pizza" is unknown. At some point, I wondered who the genius was that invented the first pizza. And surely, we all know that the tradition of this meal is Italian. But what if I told you that the history of pizza has even older roots?

The earliest traces of pizza date back to ancient Mesopotamia and classical Greece. In other words, the origins of pizza are almost as ancient as those of humankind—a truly timeless success (and it's no wonder it has lingered through the pass of time!)!
However, it is in Naples, Italy, in the 1700s, that pizza began to take the form we know and love today.
The first Neapolitan pizzaiolos started topping the flatbread with tomato and buffalo mozzarella, creating the famous "Pizza Margherita." It's the story of a simple and flavorful dish, made with humble ingredients from popular cuisine, that became a worldwide sensation.

This incredible turning point occurred with the arrival of Italians in the United States in the 19th century. Pizza started gaining popularity even overseas. The first Italian pizzerias opened in New York and Philadelphia, initially aiming to cater to the Italian community. However, their success quickly soared. The "pizza alla pala" or "pizza al taglio" emerged as a variants of pizza served in large rectangular slices. Soon, pizza spread throughout the country, becoming one of the most beloved dishes among Americans.

The United States is renowned for its unique pizza styles, such as New York-style pizza, with its thin and crispy crust, perfect for folding in half and devouring while strolling through the Big Apple. Then there's the Chicago-style pizza, with its high and crispy crust that acts as a vessel for a generous amount of cheese and toppings.
Pizza recipes are as diverse as personal preferences, local influences, and the creativity of the thousands of pizzaiolos who have delighted in creating and innovating this iconic dish loved by millions across different cultures.

Are you ready to become an expert and innovator too?
Get ready to discover all the secrets of making delicious homemade pizza and embark on a unique and gratifying experience in your kitchen. You'll be surprised to know that you don't need any fancy gadgets or specialized kitchen tools. I can assure you that one of the best pizzas I've ever eaten comes out of my Aunt Rosaria's oven every Sunday evening. It's a tradition that brings my entire family together around the table every week.

CHAPTER 1
START FROM THE BASICS

THE NECESSARY TOOLS

To start making homemade pizza, you really only need a few things: some basic ingredients, a table, a rolling pin, and an oven...

However, if you're serious about it and want to make your life easier, there are a few specific tools that could come in handy and can transform your kitchen into a small home pizzeria!

Here's a complete list of what might be useful during preparation:

- **Electronic scale:** Using a scale will allow you to weigh the ingredients precisely and achieve consistent results.
- **Food processor:** A food processor greatly simplifies and speeds up the dough preparation. This phase is undoubtedly the most labor-intensive, and it's crucial to do it well. A food processor with specific dough attachments is ideal if you want to save time and energy.
- **Bench scraper:** A bench scraper is useful for cleaning and scraping the dough off work surfaces, especially if you're preparing the dough by hand. You can also use it to divide the dough into portions and shape the pizza.
- **Rolling pin:** For manually rolling out the dough, a good rolling pin is an essential companion. Choose a high-quality wooden rolling pin, preferably with a medium diameter.
- **Pizza pans:** Pizza pans are the classic way to bake homemade pizza. They come in various sizes and materials, but I recommend to consider options like rimless baking sheets, preferably non-stick. They are perfect for rolling out the dough and baking the pizza in a home oven.
- **Pizza stone or steel plate:** As an alternative to pizza pans, you can use a pizza stone or steel plate inside the oven, which can enhance the baking quality. These materials retain heat and allow you to achieve a crispy and evenly cooked crust.
- **Dough docker:** The dough docker is an optional tool that is useful for poking holes in the dough before baking, preventing it from excessively puffing up during the baking process. Alternatively, you can use a fork.
- **Pizza peel:** A pizza peel is useful for easily inserting and removing the pizza from a wood-fired oven or an outdoor one. Make sure to choose a peel that is sized appropriately for your oven and has the right handle length.
- **Pizza cutter:** A high-quality wheel slicer with a sharp blade is the most convenient way to cut the pizza into slices when it comes out of the oven. It's a practical alternative to the classic fork and knife.
- **Serving trays:** If you want to present your pizzas in a professional and eye-catching way, consider choosing from various dedicated serving trays. The presentation will undoubtedly be even more elegant.

OVEN: EXPLORING DIFFERENT TYPES OF OVENS

The oven is certainly one of the most important elements to achieve a delicious and crispy pizza. If you have a good oven in your kitchen, that's a great starting point. For better results, it's essential to ensure even and controlled baking, so a key point is to, most importantly, know your oven. However, the electric home oven is not the only domestic way to bake pizza. Did you know, for example, that you can also do it in a skillet?

We'll delve into temperatures and baking times in a dedicated chapter later on, but for now, it's enough to know that you can prepare an extraordinary pizza in your home oven, and you don't need a wood-fired one or anything more professional. The joys of homemade pizza are truly for anyone willing to give it a try.

As you can imagine, there are many curious and alternative methods you can experiment with if you have any of these other types of ovens or devices at home:

- **Cast Iron Oven:** Cast iron ovens, such as the Dutch oven or cast iron skillets, are an excellent choice for pizza baking. Cast iron retains heat evenly and allows you to achieve a crispy crust. These can be used in both the oven and on a gas stovetop, reaching high and consistent temperatures, ideal for a good pizza.

- **Kamado-Grilled:** The kamado is a type of ceramic grill that reaches very high temperatures, ranging from 575°F to 750°F (300°C to 400°C). It is great due to its heat retention capacity. In a kamado, you can bake the pizza on a pizza stone and achieve excellent results.

- **Gas-Grilled:** Gas grills are a popular choice for outdoor pizza cooking because you can easily reach temperatures similar to those of a home oven, generally ranging from 450°F to 500°F (230°C to 260°C). With this cooking method, you can achieve a crispy crust and even baking. You will need a pizza stone or a heat-resistant non-stick pan for these.

- **Charcoal-Grilled:** Charcoal grills are also suitable for outdoor pizza baking. In addition to providing intense heat, you'll get a slight smokiness that imparts a characteristic flavor to the pizza, similar to that of a wood-fired oven. The temperatures of a charcoal grill can vary depending on the amount and arrangement of the charcoal, but they usually range around 500°F (260°C) or higher.

CHAPTER 2
THE ESSENTIAL INGREDIENTS

The foundation of pizza lies in the simplest and oldest culinary elements: flour, water, yeast, and salt. What will set your pizza apart will be your experience and the creativity you put into the toppings. However, as is often the case with simple preparations, the quality of the ingredients truly makes a difference.
That's why this chapter is one of the most important—read it attentively.

FLOUR

Flour is the key element in creating the pizza dough. There are different types of flour, each with specific characteristics that influence the texture and flavor of the dough. The most commonly used flours for pizza include:

- **Soft wheat flour:** This is the most versatile and widely-available flour. It is suitable for most pizza recipes and can be used successfully on its own or in combination with other flours.

- **Hard wheat flour:** This flour is made from wheat with a high gluten content. It has a more elastic and sturdy texture compared to soft wheat flour, making it ideal for creating a robust and resilient crust. It is particularly suitable for making thin and crispy pizzas like the New York-style pizza.

- **"00" Pizza flour:** This is a very fine flour made from high-quality grains. It is used for traditional Italian pizzas such as the Neapolitan pizza. "00" flour has a moderate gluten content and gives the dough a soft and fluffy texture. It is ideal for pizzas with thin and light crusts, like the Roman or (as I already mentioned) Neapolitan-style dough.

- **Whole wheat flour:** If you prefer a more nutritious pizza, you can opt for whole wheat flour. This flour retains the germ and bran of the grain, which are the most nutrient-rich parts. Whole wheat flour gives the pizza a more rustic texture and a distinctive flavor. However, do keep in mind that dough made with whole wheat flour may require slightly more hydration. You can experiment with a combination of whole wheat flour and "00" flour once you have gained some experience with dough-making.

- **Gluten-free flour:** For those following a gluten-free diet, there are specially formulated flours for making gluten-free pizzas. These flours can be made from rice flour, cornstarch, buckwheat, quinoa, or other gluten-free ingredients. Gluten-free dough requires slightly different handling and processing compared to traditional wheat-based dough, which we will discuss later.

The choice of flour determines the texture and type of pizza you are going to achieve. Many expert pizza makers experiment with different flour combinations to achieve customized results. If you're just starting out, stick to one of the basic recipes you'll find in the next chapter, and only when you've gained more experience should you venture into different flour combinations. You'll also discover that the amount of flour needed may vary depending on environmental and humidity conditions. The bottom line is that preparing pizza requires a bit of sensitivity and flexibility, as you'll need to adjust the amount of water and flour to achieve the desired dough consistency.

WATER

It may seem trivial, but even water can make a difference when creating the perfect pizza dough. The hydration percentage of the dough, which is the ratio of water weight to flour weight used, is a crucial factor that affects the texture and workability of the dough. The hydration percentage varies depending on the type of flour used and the desired outcome. Let's take a look at the guidelines for achieving the best results for each pizza style:

- **Classic Neapolitan Pizza:** Traditional Neapolitan pizza has a hydration percentage ranging from 60% to 70%. This relatively high hydration produces an elastic and easy-to-work-with dough. Neapolitan pizza is hand-stretched, without the need for a rolling pin, and the crust remains soft and fragrant.

- **Thin and Crispy New York-Style Pizza:** To achieve a thin and crispy pizza, it is necessary to reduce the hydration percentage to about 60 to 55%. This will give the dough a more compact and firm texture compared to Neapolitan pizza. A rolling pin is used to stretch the dough, and the result is a pizza with minimal or no crust, low and crispy.

- **Whole Wheat or Gluten-Free Pizza:** Dough made with whole wheat or gluten-free flour often requires a higher hydration than traditional doughs. The hydration percentage may vary depending on the specific recipe and type of flour used, but an increase of up to 5 to 10% compared to the general guidelines may be necessary.

Increasing the hydration percentage makes the dough moister and stickier, therefore making the handling a bit more challenging. However, it allows for a lighter and more airy crust because the dough becomes more extensible and easier to hand-stretch or roll with a rolling pin. When preparing any of these doughs, remember to add water gradually and monitor the consistency, making any necessary adjustments.

YEAST

Let's talk about yeast, this essential ingredient that performs the great magic of transforming water and flour into a soft and airy mixture. Every culture has its own traditions when it comes to yeast, and consequently, each person has their own preferences for pizza. However, the most common solution in Italy is fresh yeast (although it is not a rule). Here is a brief overview to choose from and experiment with to find your perfect recipe.

- **Fresh yeast:** It is one of the most traditional and widely-used yeasts for making pizza. It is sold in the form of a block or cube and needs to be activated before use. To activate it, simply dissolve the yeast in warm water with a teaspoon of sugar and let it rest for a few minutes until a foam forms on the surface. Fresh yeast gives the pizza a distinctive flavor and good leavening.

- **Active dry yeast:** This type of yeast is also very common in homemade pizza recipes. It is sold in the form of dry granules and does not require activation. It can be added directly to the dry ingredients of the dough. The only important note is to follow the instructions on the package regarding the quantity to use. Generally, one packet of active dry yeast (7 grams) is sufficient for a standard pizza recipe.

- **Instant yeast:** Instant yeast is similar to active dry yeast but is ground into smaller particles, making it more easily soluble. It is also known as quick-rise yeast or pizza yeast. It can be added directly to the dry ingredients of the dough and does not require activation. Instant yeast can reduce the proofing time, allowing you to prepare the pizza more quickly.

To achieve good leavening and a perfect dough, consider that the following factors also have a significant impact on the rising process:

1. Temperature: If you are using fresh yeast, make sure the water temperature used to activate the yeast is warm, generally around 35 to 40°C (95 to 104°F). Water that is too hot can damage the yeast, while water that is too cold can slow down the leavening process. In general, the ambient temperature also affects the rising process. Yeast doughs tend to rise more easily in a well-heated environment or if the dough is placed in a warm spot.

2. Resting: After preparing the dough, let it rest in a warm, draft-free place. Cover the dough with a damp cloth or plastic wrap to prevent a crust from forming on its surface. The duration of the rising process depends on the type of yeast used and the ambient temperature, but it typically takes 1 to 2 hours for a dough to double in size.

3. Handling the dough: After the rising process, handle the dough gently to avoid deflating it. Divide it into portions and shape the dough balls with light movements. Each dough ball you divide will become a pizza. Let the dough balls rest for a few minutes before stretching them into the desired shape.

SALT

Salt adds flavor to the dough and not only enhances the taste but also helps regulate the fermentation and texture of the dough. Use high-quality sea salt or kitchen salt and sprinkle it carefully—excessive salt can negatively affect the fermentation process.

SUGAR

Sugar is an optional ingredient that can be added to the dough to contribute to fermentation. It helps activate the yeast and speeds up the process. When used in small quantities—typically one or two teaspoons for a standard pizza recipe—it helps achieve a golden and well-colored crust while balancing the flavor.

PIZZA MASTER TIPS

As I mentioned before, temperature, humidity, and the environment can greatly influence the success of your homemade dough!

Preparing pizza dough is an art that requires attention to detail and an understanding of the variables that can impact the final result. In addition to the basic ingredients you choose to use, as we've already seen, temperature, humidity, and the surrounding environment can play a significant role in the texture and leavening of the dough.

The ambient temperature is one of the first things to consider when preparing your dough. In a warm environment, yeast activity intensifies, accelerating the leavening process. Conversely, in a cold environment, yeast becomes less active, and leavening takes longer. Finding a balance in ambient temperature can contribute to achieving even and controlled dough leavening.

Ambient humidity is another factor to take into account. In humid environments, the moisture in the air can interact with the flour, making the dough moister. This may require a slight reduction in the amount of water compared to the basic recipe to maintain the desired consistency.

Both temperature and ambient humidity can vary depending on the season, geographical location, and weather conditions. Therefore, the dough preparation process may require some adjustments depending on any of these factors. Everything will become easier and clearer with experience and a certain sensitivity that will develop over time.

Pizza is an art, and as such, it requires practice and patience. Enjoy the process and experimentation, and embark on this delicious journey without rushing to achieve the best right away.

CHAPTER 3
LET'S MAKE THE DOUGH!

The dough is the heart and soul of homemade pizza. It is where everything begins, where the ingredients come together and transform into a soft and fragrant mass. But the dough is more than just a simple combination of flour, water, yeast, and salt. It requires practice, experimentation, and dedication to get it to perfection. The basic recipe may be the same for everyone, but what truly makes a difference is the experience, skill, and even the sensitivity of the one kneading the dough. With time and perseverance, every dough will become more refined, and the satisfaction you feel with it will be even greater.

So, don't be afraid to experiment, to adapt the recipe to your preferences, and to add your personal touch. Let yourself be guided by instinct and passion, and soon you will realize how rewarding it is to create your own homemade pizza.

And now, let's explore together the most traditional dough bases from which you can start creating your first pizza in your own kitchen.

CLASSIC NEAPOLITAN DOUGH (HYDRATION 65%)

The classic Neapolitan dough is the foundation for the famous Neapolitan pizza, known for its soft, light, and slightly elastic crust. To prepare this dough, you will need type "00" flour, water, fresh yeast, salt, and a pinch of sugar. Here is the basic recipe for the classic Neapolitan dough:

Ingredients for 5 medium-sized pizzas:
- 2.2 lbs type "00" flour (1 kg)
- 2.75 cups water (650 ml)
- 0.25 oz fresh yeast (7g)
- 1 tbsp salt (20 g)
- 1/2 tsp sugar (2 g)

Start by dissolving the fresh yeast in room temperature water and add the sugar to help activate the yeast. In a large bowl, mix the flour and salt, then pour the yeast water into the center. Mix the ingredients until you have a homogeneous dough, then transfer it onto a lightly floured work surface.

Knead vigorously for at least 10 to 15 minutes until the dough becomes smooth and elastic. Shape the dough into a single ball and place it in a lightly oiled bowl. Cover the bowl with a damp cloth and let the dough rise for about 4 to 5 hours.

After the dough has risen, divide it into 5 uniform-sized balls, usually 6.3 to 7.1 ounces (180 to 200 grams) each, and let them rest covered for another 60 minutes. During this time, the dough will relax and become easier to stretch.

Once the balls are ready, you can stretch the dough by hand. Neapolitan pizzaioli are skilled at spinning it in the air, and the general secret is not to press it down when stretching, so using a rolling pin is not recommended.

THERE'S NOTHING BETTER THAN LEARNING BY WATCHING.
That's why I've put together a video tutorial in my kitchen, showing you how to make the perfect authentic Neapolitan pizza. I'll guide you step by step, complementing the process with my tips. You'll see how to handle the dough correctly to achieve a light, fluffy, and fragrant crust.
To access the video, simply scan the QR code at the end of the book or visit https://bit.ly/pizzavideotutorial

CLASSIC NEW YORK-STYLE DOUGH (HYDRATION 55%)

What is the secret to achieving a thin and crispy New York-style crust? The addition of an extra ingredient compared to the Neapolitan base: olive oil and a lower hydration level. The New York-style dough is firmer, and you'll need a rolling pin to roll it out. The challenge lies in achieving the thinnest possible crust!

Here's the basic recipe for 5 medium-sized pizzas:
- 2.2 lbs type "00" flour (1 kg)
- 2.25 cups water (550 ml)
- 0.25 oz fresh yeast (7g)
- 1 tbsp salt (20 g)
- 0.25 cup olive oil (60 ml)

Start by dissolving the fresh yeast in room temperature water. In a large bowl, mix the flour and salt, then add the water with the yeast and the olive oil. Mix the ingredients until you obtain a homogeneous dough.

Transfer the dough onto a lightly floured work surface and knead vigorously for about 10 to 15 minutes, until it becomes smooth and elastic. Shape the dough into a ball and place it in a lightly oiled bowl. Cover the bowl with a damp cloth and let the dough rise at room temperature for about 1 to 2 hours.

Once the dough has risen, divide it into 5 uniform-sized balls, usually around 6.3 to 7.1 ounces (180 to 200 grams) each. Roll each of them out on a lightly oiled pizza pan or baking sheet and top them with your favorite ingredients.

CHICAGO-STYLE DOUGH

The Chicago-style or Deep Dish Pizza is an American recipe from Chicago that's renowned worldwide. It has nothing to do with Italian pizza as it features a different dough and is much thicker (resembling more of a pie than a pizza). The toppings are also arranged differently, with the mozzarella in direct contact with the crust, followed by the other toppings, and finally the tomato sauce and Parmesan cheese.

Here are the ingredients to make 2 pizzas:
- 8.8 oz bread flour (250 g)
- 2.3 oz cornmeal (65 g)
- 1 tsp dry yeast
- 1 tsp granulated sugar
- 4.7 fluid ounces warm water (140 ml)
- 1 teaspoon salt
- 0.5 ounces melted butter (15 g)
- 1 tbsp extra-virgin olive oil

In a bowl, combine the warm water, dry yeast, and granulated sugar. Stir well until the ingredients dissolve, and let it rest for 5 minutes.

In another bowl, mix the bread flour and cornmeal thoroughly with a spoon. Gradually add the water mixture, melted butter, and finally the salt. Knead the dough until it becomes smooth and homogeneous. Shape it into a ball and place it in a bowl. Grease the dough well with olive oil and let it rise for 60 minutes, covering the bowl with plastic wrap. If you want to speed up the process, you can place the bowl in the oven with only the light turned on.

Once the dough has risen, roll it out and line a greased 22-inch diameter pan. The dough should cover the edges of the pan. At this point, you can proceed with the toppings. Chicago-style pizza requires a longer baking time, approximately 20 to 25 minutes.

FOCACCIA DOUGH

Focaccia is like a mouthwatering blend of soft bread and flavorful pizza, an Italian recipe that has made its way across the globe. When Italians make homemade pizza, it often leans more towards a delicious focaccia rather than the traditional round pie. That's why it seems like a fantastic idea to include this dough recipe in the book.

Preparing focaccia is a breeze and can bring great satisfaction even to those starting out in the kitchen. Typically baked in rectangular pans and cut into squares, it's perfect as an appetizer or can even be used as a bread alternative for tasty sandwiches. What sets it apart is the dough—it's thicker, fluffier, and infused with olive oil, resulting in a delightful, aromatic treat. And don't forget, just like a pizza, you can top and bake it with a variety of ingredients.

The beauty of focaccia lies in its versatility, making it a must-try for anyone seeking culinary bliss. Trust me, once you've experienced the wonders of fresh, homemade focaccia, you'll be hooked!

Ingredients:
- 4 cups durum wheat flour
- 1.25 cups water
- 0.25 oz fresh yeast (7g)
- 2 tsp of salt
- 0.25 cup extra-virgin olive oil

Start by dissolving the fresh yeast in warm water and let it rest for a few minutes until it becomes frothy. In a large bowl, pour the durum wheat flour and add the activated yeast. Add the salt and extra-virgin olive oil and mix the ingredients with a spatula or your hands until they form a homogeneous dough.

Transfer the dough to a lightly floured surface and knead it vigorously for about 10 minutes until it becomes smooth and elastic. Shape the dough into a ball and place it in a lightly oiled bowl. Cover with a damp cloth and let it rise in a warm place for about 1 to 2 hours or until it doubles in size.

Once the dough has risen, take it out and flatten it with your hands on an oiled baking sheet. Cover the baking sheet with a damp cloth and let it rise for another 30 to 45 minutes.

Preheat the oven to 425°F (220°C) while it rises.
Bake the focaccia for about 20 to 25 minutes or until it turns golden and crispy. Once it's baked, remove the focaccia from the oven and let it cool slightly before cutting it into slices and serving.

WHOLE WHEAT DOUGH

Whole wheat dough is made with 100% whole wheat flour or a mixture of whole wheat flour and traditional white flour. This dough will have a rustic, fragrant flavor. It's a variation of the classic homemade pizza dough but richer in fiber, with a crispy exterior and a soft interior.

Here's the basic recipe for 5 medium-sized pizzas:
- 1.76 lbs whole wheat flour (800 g)
- 7.05 oz type "00" flour (200 g)
- 2.96 cups water (700 ml)
- 0.1 oz fresh yeast (3 g)
- 0.25 cup olive oil (60 ml)
- 0.7 oz salt (20 g)
- 1 tsp sugar

Start by dissolving the fresh yeast in room temperature water, also adding the sugar. In a bowl, mix both types of flour and the salt. Pour the yeast water into the center and mix until you have a homogeneous dough.

Transfer the dough to a lightly floured work surface and knead it vigorously for about 10 to 15 minutes, until it becomes smooth and elastic. Shape the dough into a ball and place it in a lightly oiled bowl. Cover the bowl with a damp cloth and let the dough rise for about 2 to 3 hours, or until it doubles in size.

After the dough has risen, you can divide it into 5 portions and roll them out one by one using a rolling pin.

Whole wheat dough usually requires slightly longer baking compared to classic dough, so keep it in the oven for a slightly longer time.

GLUTEN-FREE DOUGH

For those following a gluten-free diet, it is possible to prepare a delicious pizza using alternative gluten-free flours.

Here's a basic recipe for five gluten-free pizzas:
- 10.6 oz rice flour (300 g)
- 7.1 oz cornflour (200 g)
- 3.5 oz potato starch (100 g)
- 1.38 cups water (325 ml)
- 0.35 oz fresh yeast (10 g)
- 0.35 oz salt (10 g)
- 1 tsp sugar

Dissolve the fresh yeast in room temperature water, adding the sugar to aid yeast activation. In a bowl, mix the gluten-free flours and salt. Pour the yeast water into the center and mix until you have a homogeneous dough.

Transfer the dough to a lightly floured work surface using gluten-free flour and knead vigorously for about 10 to 15 minutes, until it becomes smooth and elastic. Shape the dough into a ball and place it in a lightly oiled bowl.
Cover the bowl with a damp cloth and let the dough rise for about 1 yo 2 hours, or until it doubles in size.

After the dough has risen, roll it out on a lightly oiled pizza pan and top it with your preferred gluten-free ingredients.
Gluten-Free dough usually requires slightly longer baking compared to classic dough, so keep it in the oven for a slightly longer time.

Before rolling out the dough and proceeding to the next steps, it is crucial to ensure that the proofing phase is completed and the dough has reached the right level of maturity. It may not be easy to determine this at first, so here are some tips and techniques to know if the dough is truly ready:

- **Check its volume:** During the proofing phase, the dough should increase in volume. You can assess if it has proofed enough simply by evaluating how much space it occupies inside the container. Generally, the dough is ready to be rolled out when it has doubled in size.

- **Verify the consistency**: A well-proofed classic dough should be soft, elastic, and easily workable. If the dough feels too stiff or excessively sticky, it may need some more proofing time.

- **Try the finger test:** Perform a small test by gently pressing a finger into the center of the dough. If the indentation springs back quickly without leaving a fingerprint, the dough is not yet ready. However, if it springs back slowly and leaves a slight imprint, the proofing is perfect.

- **Windowpane test:** Take a small piece of dough and gently stretch it between your fingers. If you can form a thin, stretchy membrane without it breaking easily, it means the dough has matured sufficiently. This test is particularly useful for highly hydrated dough, such as Neapolitan pizza dough.

- **Observe the bubbles:** During proofing, the dough should develop bubbles on the inside. You can observe the presence of these bubbles on the dough's surface. If you notice many bubbles, it means the dough has proofed correctly.

Remember that the proofing time may vary based on room temperature, humidity, and the ingredients used. It is important to observe the dough closely, and practice and experience will help you refine your ability to determine the right timing to proceed.

FLAWLESS PIZZA ROLLOUT

To properly roll out the dough, follow these steps:

1. Prepare a clean and floured work surface. You can use a lightly floured countertop or a baking board.

2. Take the dough and shape it into a ball with your hands. Transfer it onto the floured surface.

3. With lightly floured hands, start pressing the dough from the center outwards to distribute the air evenly.

4. Use your thumbs and hands to exert gentle pressure on the dough, pushing it outward in a circular motion. You can rotate the dough occasionally to ensure it is rolled out evenly.

5. Continue rolling out the dough until you achieve the desired size. You can make a traditional round pizza or a rectangular shape for focaccia.

6. While rolling, check the elasticity of the dough. If the dough shrinks back or springs back to its original shape, let it rest for a few minutes, then continue rolling. For Neapolitan or whole wheat dough, you should be able to simply stretch the pizza by hand, while for other types of dough, you can use a rolling pin for assistance.

7. Once the dough is rolled out, transfer it onto a lightly floured baking tray, a lightly oiled pizza peel, or a baking stone, depending on your chosen baking method.

PIZZA MASTER TIPS

- **Be patient:** Handle the dough with care, avoiding excessive pressure. A delicately treated dough retains its structure and consistency during baking.

- **Let the dough rest:** After rolling out the dough, let it rest for a few minutes before adding the toppings. This allows the dough to relax and adjust to the given shape.

- **Adjust the temperature:** Ensure that your dough and ingredients are at room temperature. Dough that is too cold can be more difficult to roll out.

- **Use a rolling pin or your hands:** You can roll out the dough using a rolling pin or simply your hands. Choose the method you feel most comfortable with to achieve the best results.

- **Experiment with thickness:** You can adjust the thickness of the dough according to your personal preferences. A thinner pizza will have a crispier crust, while a thicker one will be softer.

- **Flour your tools:** To prevent the dough from sticking to the tool used for rolling, such as a rolling pin or your hands, make sure to lightly flour it.

- **Maintain the shape:** During rolling, regularly check the shape of the dough to ensure it is even and hasn't spread too much.

- **Final resting time:** After topping the pizza, let it rest for a couple of minutes more before baking.

CHAPTER 5
SAUCES

After all the effort you've put into the dough and fermentation, your pizza truly deserves the best. Let's talk about sauces, toppings, and all those ingredients that will transform your pizza into a true masterpiece of taste and creativity!

CLASSIC TOMATO SAUCE

Tomato sauce is the classic base for pizza, the true and authentic Italian recipe. In Italy, they don't like to use too many toppings; the Margherita pizza is the true queen of pizzas, but for it to be truly unforgettable, it's essential that both the dough and the tomato sauce be sensational. You can make the sauce at home using San Marzano tomatoes, or you can buy a ready-made one, but don't skimp on quality. Trust me, good sauce makes a difference. In Italy, every pizza maker has their own sauce recipe, and traditionally the sauce is also made at home within the family. During the summer when tomatoes reach their peak ripeness, they are harvested or purchased in large quantities, and one or two days are dedicated to preparing and bottling the sauce that will last throughout the year.

Believe me, sauce in Italy is a serious matter! Here's a simple recipe to learn how to prepare it and give your pizza an extra boost!

Here is the traditional recipe for Italian Tomato Sauce:

Ingredients:
- 14 oz ripe tomatoes (preferably San Marzano) (400g)
- 2 tbsp extra-virgin olive oil
- 1 clove garlic (optional)
- 1 tsp salt
- Black pepper - to taste
- A few leaves of fresh basil

Peel the tomatoes and remove the seeds. Cut them into cubes or roughly chop them.
In a pan, heat the olive oil and add the garlic (if you want a touch of flavor). Cook the garlic until it turns golden, then remove it.
Add the tomatoes to the pan and let them cook over medium-low heat for about 15-20 minutes, until they become thick and soft. Lightly crush them with a fork to achieve a smoother consistency.
Season with salt and black pepper to taste. Add some fresh basil leaves to give a touch of freshness to the sauce.
Let the tomato sauce cool before using it as a base for your pizzas.

PESTO GENOVESE

Pesto Genovese is an aromatic and flavorful sauce, perfect for adding a touch of freshness to your pizza. In Italy, it is often used on focaccia, which is a white pizza without tomato sauce. It is a less commonly-used sauce compared to traditional tomato sauce, but when freshly prepared, it will give your pizza an intense, fragrant, and summery taste.

Here is the traditional recipe for Pesto Genovese:

Ingredients:
- 1.8 oz fresh basil (50g)
- 1.1 oz pine nuts (30g)
- 1.1 oz grated Parmesan cheese (30g)
- 1.1 oz grated Pecorino cheese (30g)
- 1 clove garlic
- 3.4 fl oz extra-virgin olive oil (100ml)
- 1 tsp salt

In a mortar, crush the garlic clove together with the pine nuts until you obtain a smooth paste.
Add the fresh basil and continue crushing until the basil crumbles.
Add the grated Parmesan cheese and grated Pecorino cheese. Keep crushing until you get a thick sauce.
Gradually add the olive oil while continuing to crush until you achieve a creamy consistency.
Adjust the salt according to your taste. Make sure to taste the pesto to adjust the flavor intensity.
Store the Pesto Genovese in an airtight jar, covered with a layer of olive oil, in the refrigerator until ready to use.

ALFREDO SAUCE

The famous Alfredo sauce can also be used as a pizza topping. Its creamy consistency and rich cheese flavor make it a delicious choice to enhance the other toppings you use. You can spread it on the pizza base instead of traditional tomato sauce and add your favorite ingredients such as chicken, bacon, mushrooms, spinach, or various cheeses. The combination of a crispy crust, Alfredo sauce, and tasty toppings creates an irresistible gourmet pizza.

Here's how to prepare it:

Ingredients:
- 0.5 cup unsalted butter
- 1 cup heavy cream
- 1 cup grated Parmigiano Reggiano cheese
- Salt, to taste
- Freshly ground white pepper, to taste
- Grated nutmeg, to taste (optional)

In a medium saucepan over medium heat, melt the butter until completely liquid.

Add the heavy cream and stir well with a wooden spoon or whisk.

Continue cooking over medium-low heat, stirring constantly, until the cream is heated through without boiling.

Add the grated Parmigiano Reggiano cheese and continue stirring until it melts completely and the sauce becomes smooth and creamy.

Taste the sauce and season with salt and freshly ground white pepper to your liking. If desired, you can also add a light sprinkle of grated nutmeg for an extra flavor boost.

Remove the sauce from the heat and let it cool slightly before using it as a topping for your pizza.

You can store any leftover Alfredo sauce in an airtight container in the refrigerator for a couple of days. Before using it again, gently heat it over low heat, stirring to bring it back to the desired creamy consistency.

DO NOT TELL AN ITALIAN!

As mentioned earlier, Italians are very attached to traditional ingredients when it comes to pizza, and you will never find a pizzeria in Italy that offers alternative sauces like the ones I'm about to list. However, everyone has their own tastes, and pizza knows no boundaries... in international cuisine, it's not uncommon to find someone who flavors their pizza with these sauces:

- **Barbecue Sauce:** Originating from the United States, barbecue sauce adds a smoky and sweet touch to pizza. It's perfect for enhancing pizzas with meat, chicken, or smoked ingredients.

- **Seafood Sauce:** In some coastal regions, such as parts of Southern Italy, it's common to use a seafood-based sauce to flavor pizza. This sauce, enriched with calamari, shrimp, mussels, and clams, gives a delicious and sea-like taste to the pizza.

- **Spicy Sauce:** For spice lovers, spicy sauce is an excellent choice to give a lively kick to pizza. You can use a commercial spicy sauce or create your own homemade sauce with chili peppers, chili powder, or other spicy ingredients. Generally, in Italy, a drizzle of spicy oil is added raw to the pizza.

- **Sweet and Sour Sauce:** In some Asian cuisines, like Chinese cuisine, sweet and sour sauce is used to flavor pizza. This sauce combines sweet and acidic flavors, creating an interesting taste contrast.

- **Tzatziki Sauce:** Of Greek origin, tzatziki sauce made with yogurt, cucumber, garlic, and herbs is a fresh and light choice for pizza seasoning. It's particularly suitable for pizzas with ingredients like chicken, lamb, or grilled vegetables.

- **Mushroom Sauce:** For mushroom lovers, a sauce made with porcini or champignon mushrooms can add an earthy and rich flavor to pizza. You can use a ready-made mushroom sauce or create your own version, harnessing the creaminess and aroma of fresh mushrooms.

These are just some of the sauces you can consider for seasoning your pizza. Let yourself be inspired by international cuisine and harness your creativity to create unique and surprising flavor combinations!

CHAPTER 6
TOPPINGS AND FILLINGS

MOZZARELLA

Mozzarella is one of the most beloved and widely used cheeses in pizza preparation. It is a stretched-curd cheese that stands out for its creamy texture and delicate flavor. There are different types of mozzarella, each with its distinctive characteristics that add a unique touch to pizza.

Buffalo mozzarella DOP from Campania is considered the king of mozzarella. Made from buffalo milk, it has a rich flavor and a soft texture. Its outer surface is slightly rough, while the inside is creamy and stringy. Buffalo mozzarella is highly regarded for its quality and pairs perfectly with traditional Margherita pizza.

Stracciatella is another variety of mozzarella that deserves a special mention. It is a creamy and stringy heart, obtained by manually separating the strands of cheese. Its soft texture and delicate flavor make it perfect for topping pizzas like Caprese, where a creamy and enveloping effect is desired.

Burrata is another cheese that has gained popularity in recent years. It consists of an outer shell of mozzarella and a filling of cream and stracciatella. Its creamy texture and rich taste make it an excellent choice for enhancing pizza. Burrata can be sliced and placed on top of the pizza or spread on the crust to create a creamy topping.

In addition to these main varieties, there are several other types of mozzarella available. **Fior di latte mozzarella**, for example, is made from cow's milk and is characterized by a delicate flavor and a slightly more compact texture compared to buffalo mozzarella. Lactose-free mozzarella is designed for those who are lactose intolerant but still want to enjoy a pizza with stretchy mozzarella.

Choosing the right mozzarella for your pizza will depend on your personal preferences and the type of pizza you want to make. If you want to achieve an authentic Neapolitan pizza, buffalo mozzarella DOP from Campania is the ideal choice. If you prefer a creamier texture, stracciatella or burrata will be perfect. And if you have specific dietary needs, you can opt for lactose-free mozzarella.

Regardless of the type of mozzarella chosen, make sure to always use a high-quality one to achieve maximum flavor and a stretchy texture. Mozzarella is one of the few key ingredients for a delicious pizza, and experimenting with different varieties will allow you to create unique and satisfying flavor combinations.

CHEESES

In addition to mozzarella, there are many other Italian cheeses that can be used to top pizzas. Among the most common are grated Parmigiano Reggiano, Pecorino Romano, Gorgonzola, Provolone, Taleggio, and smoked Scamorza.

However, the variety of flavors and possibilities is truly endless, and every country has its own cheeses. Cheesy pizzas are certainly among the most appreciated, so let's not forget about cheddar cheese, goat cheese, feta cheese, blue cheese, and Fontina cheese. If you're a cheese lover, you can experiment with different combinations each time to find your favorite.

VEGETARIAN INGREDIENTS

For vegetarian pizzas, there are many topping options. You can use fresh vegetables such as tomatoes, bell peppers, onions, mushrooms, olives, beans, eggplants, and zucchini. Additionally, you can add basil leaves, arugula, spinach, or parsley to give a touch of freshness. The possibilities are endless with them raw, and you can also grill the vegetables to add more flavor. Try mixing the ingredients with creativity, and you'll achieve colorful, tasty, and flavorful vegetarian pizzas like never before!

MEAT INGREDIENTS

Meat is also a highly regarded ingredient in pizza preparation, as it adds flavor and texture. Here are some commonly-used meat ingredients for topping pizzas.

Salami: Salami is a classic meat ingredient used for pizza. There are different varieties, such as spicy salami, sweet salami, or smoked salami, each with its distinctive flavor. Sliced thin or diced, salami adds a touch of taste and pleasant crunchiness to the pizza.

Prosciutto: Prosciutto is another popular meat ingredient for pizza. The most common variety is prosciutto crudo, sliced thin and added to the pizza after baking. Its salty and delicate flavor pairs well with other ingredients like mushrooms or arugula.

Pancetta: Smoked or fresh pancetta is an excellent choice to enrich the pizza with its deep flavor and characteristic smoky taste. Diced or sliced into strips, pancetta adds a note of crispiness and a bold flavor to the pizza.

Sausage: Sausage is often used as a pizza topping, both in sweet and spicy varieties. It can be crumbled or sliced and spread over the pizza for a meaty and succulent taste. Spicy sausage adds a peppery kick that can bring vibrancy to the pizza.

Chicken: Cooked or grilled chicken is a lighter option for meat lovers. Diced or sliced chicken can be arranged on the pizza for a touch of protein-rich flavor. It can also be seasoned with spices or marinated to add even more flavor.

Bresaola: Bresaola is a dried meat, typically made from beef, that is thinly sliced and used as a topping for pizza. Its intense and slightly salty flavor pairs well with ingredients like goat cheese or arugula.

SEAFOOD INGREDIENTS

For seafood pizzas, you can use a variety of fish and seafood ingredients. Squid, shrimp, mussels, clams, tuna, smoked salmon, and anchovies are just some of the ingredients you can consider. Add a touch of lemon, parsley, or aromatic herbs and you'll enhance the seafood flavors even more.

SWEET INGREDIENTS AND FRUITS

For sweet pizzas or to create a flavor contrast, you can use sweet ingredients and fruits. For example, you can add dark or milk chocolate, hazelnut spread, honey, jam, or fresh fruits like strawberries, apples, pears, kiwi, or pineapple to your dough. These ingredients will give a sweet and surprising note to your pizza.

Pizza baking can be done using various types of ovens, each with its own characteristics and advantages. Let's start with the most common option: the home oven.

HOME OVEN AND COOKING TIPS

Baking pizza in a home oven is a common option for homemade pizza enthusiasts. To achieve optimal baking, it is helpful to have a good understanding of your own oven's functions and capabilities.

Firstly, make sure to preheat the oven to the maximum temperature provided, which usually ranges from 450°F to 500°F (230°C to 260°C). This will allow the oven to reach the necessary heat for even cooking and to achieve a crispy crust. Using a pizza stone or a baking stone inside the oven is a recommended option. These accessories help maintain a constant temperature and distribute heat evenly on the pizza's surface, promoting the formation of a crispy and golden crust.

During baking, it is advisable to check the pizza regularly to prevent it from burning or cooking unevenly. You can rotate the baking sheet or pizza stone halfway through baking to ensure even browning. Also, keep in mind that baking times may vary depending on the size and thickness of the dough, as well as the ingredients used.

Another important aspect is the positioning of the oven rack. If you prefer a crispier bottom crust, place the rack on the lower part of the oven. If you prefer even cooking on both sides, position the rack in the center of the oven. Experimenting with different rack positions and observing the results will help you find the desired level of doneness according to your personal taste.

Knowing your oven well and understanding its characteristics will help you make the most of it and achieve a delicious and well-baked pizza. Experiment with different temperature settings, rack positions, and baking times to find the perfect combination for your homemade pizzas.

However, the home electric oven is not the only option, as we have already seen at the beginning of the book. You might become passionate enough over time to want to set up a wood-fired oven in your backyard or use grills and other ovens that you normally use for BBQ. Moreover, you are about to discover that you don't even need an oven to make a good pizza; a skillet might be enough!

Whichever way you decide to bake your pizza, remember that there are two fundamental factors for successful baking:

Temperature: Obviously, this is a crucial factor in achieving a perfect pizza. Make sure to properly preheat the oven or cooking method you are using. Adequate temperature allows for even cooking, creating a crispy crust and optimal cooking of the ingredients.

Throughout the baking time, ensure that the temperature remains as constant as possible. For example, avoid opening the oven multiple times during baking and try to do so only when it's the right time to remove your pizza.

Baking time: The time you'll need to bake your pizza varies depending on the type of oven and the thickness of the dough. It is important to monitor the pizza closely during baking to prevent it from burning or remaining raw. Ideally, try to do this without opening the oven, or at least minimizing the number of times you do so. Over time, you will know your oven well enough to be able to determine how many minutes it takes to achieve your perfect pizza.

THE 7 RULES FOR THE PERFECT PIZZA

1. Use high-quality ingredients: Choose fresh and high-quality ingredients to ensure the best flavor and texture for your pizza.

2. Spread the dough evenly: Make sure to spread the dough evenly, without any thicker or thinner areas. This will contribute to an even pizza cooking.

3. Moderate the amount of toppings: Avoid overloading the pizza with toppings. Using too many ingredients can make the dough soggy and difficult to cook properly.

4. Distribute toppings evenly: Distribute the toppings evenly on the pizza to prevent them from accumulating in one spot.

5. Experiment with flavor combinations: Don't be afraid to experiment with new combinations. Play with different seasonings, cheeses, and ingredients to create your unique and delicious pizza.

6. Bake and let it rest: Once the pizza is ready, take it out of the oven and let it rest for a few minutes before cutting. This allows the flavors to meld together and the crust to set.

7. Enjoy your pizza: Lastly, take the time to savor your pizza. Sit down, relax, and enjoy every bite of this homemade creation.

CHAPTER 8
TROUBLESHOOTING: COMMON PROBLEM RESOLUTION

Despite your efforts, you may encounter some issues while preparing homemade pizzas. Here is a list of the most common problems people have, and their possible solutions:

- Dough Too Sticky or Difficult to Work With
If the dough is too sticky or difficult to work with, you may need to add some extra flour during the kneading phase. Gradually add flour until you achieve the desired consistency. Also, make sure to work on a lightly floured surface to prevent the dough from sticking.

- Dough Too Dry or Difficult to Roll Out
If the dough is too dry or difficult to roll out, you may need to add a little water during the kneading phase. Gradually add water until you get a soft and easily workable dough. If the dough has already been divided into balls, you can also slightly moisten your hands while rolling it out.

- Dough Not Rising or Rising Too Slow
If the dough doesn't rise or rises slowly, it may be due to the room temperature. Make sure to create a warm and cozy environment for your dough during the rising phase. You can place the dough in a warm spot like the turned-off oven with the light on or near a heat source. Alternatively, you could increase the amount of yeast in the recipe or extend the rising times.

- Crust Too Thin or Too Thick
If your pizza crust turns out too thin or too thick, you may need to adjust the dough thickness while rolling it out. Pay attention to spread the dough evenly, maintaining a consistent thickness across the entire surface. Experiment with different amounts of dough to achieve the desired texture.

- Burnt Crust or Unevenly Cooked Toppings
If the pizza crust burns before the toppings are evenly cooked, you may need to adjust the baking temperature or time. Lower the oven temperature or reduce the baking time to avoid a burnt crust. Also, make sure to distribute the toppings evenly on the pizza to ensure correct cooking.

- Pizza Collapsing in the Center
If the pizza collapses in the center during baking, you may need to adjust the amount of toppings used. Too many moist toppings can make the dough heavy and cause it to collapse in the center. Try reducing the amount of moist toppings or pre-cook any ingredients that release a lot of water, such as leafy greens, before adding them to the pizza.

Remember that practice and experimentation are key to improving your skills. Don't get discouraged if you encounter difficulties; continue to have fun and enjoy the process of creating your artisanal pizza.

Now that we've covered everything you need to know to start making excellent homemade pizzas, it's time to unleash your creativity. Here are +100 different pizza recipes for you, ranging from traditional Italian ones to extravagant and innovative options.

Don't limit yourself, have fun experimenting, and enjoy your meal!

THE ITALIAN STYLE

The 20 recipes in this section are the most classic Italian pizzas. They are traditional recipes, and that's why I prefer to keep their original names without translation.

Italian pizza is usually of two types: with Neapolitan-style dough, or Roman-style dough, which is thinner and crispier.

Roman-style dough is quite similar to New York-style, so you can try these recipes with both versions and achieve a true Italian pizza.

You will notice that these recipes have few toppings because Italians enjoy the harmony of individual flavors and avoid excessive mixing. As a result, each ingredient holds great importance. Choose an excellent sauce for the Margherita pizza, or even make it at home following the traditional recipe we have seen before. Needless to say, good-quality mozzarella makes a huge difference... in short, these minimal recipes focus mostly on the quality and authenticity of the ingredients.

Classic Neapolitan-style Dough Recipe

Ingredients:
- 2.2 lbs type "00" flour (1 kg)
- 2.75 cups water (650 ml)
- 0.25 oz fresh yeast (7g)
- 1 tbsp salt (20 g)
- 1/2 tsp sugar (2 g)

Start by dissolving the fresh yeast in room temperature water and add the sugar to help activate the yeast. In a large bowl, mix the flour and salt, then pour the yeast water into the center. Mix the ingredients until you have a homogeneous dough, then transfer it onto a lightly floured work surface.

Knead vigorously for at least 10 to 15 minutes until the dough becomes smooth and elastic. Shape the dough into a single ball and place it in a lightly oiled bowl. Cover the bowl with a damp cloth and let the dough rise for about 4 to 5 hours.

After the dough has risen, divide it into 5 uniform-sized balls, usually 6.3 to 7.1 ounces (180 to 200 grams) each, and let them rest covered for another 60 minutes. During this time, the dough will relax and become easier to stretch.

Once the balls are ready, you can stretch the dough by hand. Neapolitan pizzaioli are skilled at spinning it in the air, and the general secret is not to press it down when stretching, so using a rolling pin is not recommended.

MARGHERITA

Dough Recipe
Classic Neapolitan-Style

Ingredients

- Pizza dough (Neapolitan-style), ready to use
- Tomato sauce
- Mozzarella cheese
- Fresh basil leaves

Nutritional Values
(per pizza, approximate)

- 900 cal
- Carbohydrates: 100g
- Protein: 35g
- Fat: 35g

Preparation

1. Preheat your oven to the highest temperature possible (usually around 500°F or 260°C).
2. On a floured surface, roll out the pizza dough into a round disc, about 10 to 12 inches (25 to 30 cm) in diameter.
3. Transfer the rolled-out dough to a pizza peel or a baking sheet lined with parchment paper.
4. Spread a layer of tomato sauce evenly over the dough, leaving a small border around the edges.
5. Sprinkle an ample amount of mozzarella cheese over the sauce.
6. Cook the pizza in the preheated oven for approximately 10 to 12 minutes, or until the crust is golden and crispy, and the cheese is melted and nicely browned.
7. Remove the pizza from the oven and let it cool for a few minutes. Garnish with fresh basil leaves.
8. Slice and serve hot.

MARINARA

Dough Recipe
Classic Neapolitan-Style

Ingredients

- Pizza dough (Neapolitan-style), ready to use
- Tomato sauce
- Garlic cloves, minced
- Dried oregano
- Extra-virgin olive oil
- Salt

Nutritional Values
(per pizza, approximate)

- 800 cal
- Carbohydrates: 90g
- Protein: 35g
- Fat: 30g

Preparation

1. Preheat your oven to the highest temperature possible (usually around 500°F or 260°C).
2. On a floured surface, roll out the pizza dough into a round disc, about 10 to 12 inches (25 to 30 cm) in diameter.
3. Transfer the rolled-out dough to a pizza peel or a baking sheet lined with parchment paper.
4. Spread a layer of tomato sauce evenly over the dough, leaving a small border around the edges.
5. Sprinkle minced garlic, dried oregano, and a drizzle of extra-virgin olive oil over the sauce.
6. Season with salt to taste.
7. Bake the pizza in the preheated oven for about 10 to 12 minutes until the crust is golden brown.
8. Remove the pizza from the oven and let it cool for a few minutes.
9. Slice and serve hot.

NAPOLETANA

Dough Recipe
Classic Neapolitan-Style

Ingredients

- Pizza dough (Neapolitan-style), ready to use
- Tomato sauce
- Mozzarella cheese
- Anchovy fillets
- Capers
- Fresh oregano leaves
- Extra-virgin olive oil

Nutritional Values
(per pizza, approximate)

- 900 cal
- Carbohydrates: 100g
- Protein: 30g
- Fat: 35g

Preparation

1. Preheat your oven to the highest temperature possible (usually around 500°F or 260°C).
2. On a floured surface, roll out the pizza dough into a round disc, about 10 to 12 inches (25 to 30 cm) in diameter.
3. Transfer the rolled-out dough to a pizza peel or a baking sheet lined with parchment paper.
4. Spread a layer of tomato sauce evenly over the dough, leaving a small border around the edges.
5. Arrange anchovy fillets and capers over the sauce.
6. Sprinkle fresh oregano leaves on top.
7. Drizzle with extra-virgin olive oil.
8. Cook the pizza in the preheated oven for approximately 10 to 12 minutes, or until the crust is golden and crispy, and the cheese is melted and nicely browned.
9. Remove the pizza from the oven and let it cool for a few minutes.
10. Slice and serve hot.

QUATTRO STAGIONI

Dough Recipe
Classic Neapolitan-Style

Ingredients

- Pizza dough (Neapolitan-style), ready to use
- Tomato sauce
- Mozzarella cheese
- Cooked ham, sliced
- Mushrooms, sliced
- Artichoke hearts, quartered
- Black olives, pitted and halved

Nutritional Values
(per pizza, approximate)

- 1000 cal
- Carbohydrates: 110g
- Protein: 35g
- Fat: 40g

Preparation

1. Preheat your oven to the highest temperature possible (usually around 500°F or 260°C).
2. On a floured surface, roll out the pizza dough into a round disc, about 10 to 12 inches (25 to 30 cm) in diameter.
3. Transfer the rolled-out dough to a pizza peel or a baking sheet lined with parchment paper.
4. Spread a layer of tomato sauce evenly over the dough, leaving a small border around the edges.
5. Divide the pizza into four quadrants.
6. In one quadrant, arrange slices of cooked ham.
7. In another quadrant, distribute sliced mushrooms.
8. In the third quadrant, place quartered artichoke hearts.
9. In the fourth quadrant, scatter halved black olives.
10. Sprinkle an ample amount of mozzarella cheese over the entire pizza.
11. Bake the pizza in the preheated oven for about 10 to 12 minutes until the crust is golden brown and the cheese is melted.
12. Remove the pizza from the oven and let it cool for a few minutes. Slice and serve hot.

CAPRICCIOSA

Dough Recipe
Classic Neapolitan-Style

Ingredients

- Pizza dough (Neapolitan-style), ready to use
- Tomato sauce
- Mozzarella cheese
- Cooked ham, sliced
- Mushrooms, sliced
- Artichoke hearts, quartered
- Black olives, pitted and halved
- Olive oil
- Salt
- Fresh basil leaves (optional)

Nutritional Values
(per pizza, approximate)

- 1000 cal
- Carbohydrates: 110g
- Protein: 35g
- Fat: 40g

Preparation

1. Preheat your oven to the highest temperature possible (usually around 500°F or 260°C).
2. On a floured surface, roll out the pizza dough into a round disc, about 10 to 12 inches (25 to 30 cm) in diameter.
3. Transfer the rolled-out dough to a pizza peel or a baking sheet lined with parchment paper.
4. Spread a layer of tomato sauce evenly over the dough, leaving a small border around the edges.
5. Distribute sliced cooked ham, mushrooms, quartered artichoke hearts and halved black olives over the sauce.
6. Drizzle with a little olive oil and sprinkle with a pinch of salt.
7. Sprinkle an ample amount of mozzarella cheese over the toppings.
8. Cook the pizza in the preheated oven for approximately 10 to 12 minutes, or until the crust is golden and crispy, and the cheese is melted and nicely browned.
9. Remove the pizza from the oven and let it cool for a few minutes.
10. If desired, garnish with fresh basil leaves.
11. Slice and serve hot.

DIAVOLA

Dough Recipe
Classic Neapolitan-Style

Ingredients

- Pizza dough (Neapolitan-style), ready to use
- Tomato sauce
- Mozzarella cheese
- Spicy salami, sliced
- Red chili flakes (optional)
- Fresh basil leaves (optional)

Nutritional Values
(per pizza, approximate)

- 1000 cal
- Carbohydrates: 100g
- Protein: 35g
- Fat: 40g

Preparation

1. Preheat your oven to the highest temperature possible (usually around 500°F or 260°C).
2. On a floured surface, roll out the pizza dough into a round disc, about 10 to 12 inches (25 to 30 cm) in diameter.
3. Transfer the rolled-out dough to a pizza peel or a baking sheet lined with parchment paper.
4. Spread a layer of tomato sauce evenly over the dough, leaving a small border around the edges.
5. Arrange slices of spicy salami over the sauce.
6. If desired, sprinkle red chili flakes to add extra heat.
7. Sprinkle an ample amount of mozzarella cheese over the toppings.
8. Bake the pizza in the preheated oven for about 10 to 12 minutes until the crust is golden brown and the cheese is melted and bubbly.
9. Remove the pizza from the oven and let it cool for a few minutes.
10. If desired, garnish with fresh basil leaves.
11. Slice and serve hot.

QUATTRO FORMAGGI

Dough Recipe
Classic Neapolitan-Style

Ingredients
- Pizza dough (Neapolitan-style), ready to use
- Tomato sauce
- Mozzarella cheese
- Gorgonzola cheese
- Parmesan cheese
- Fontina cheese

Nutritional Values
(per pizza, approximate)
- 1100 cal
- Carbohydrates: 115g
- Protein: 40g
- Fat: 50g

Preparation
1. Preheat your oven to the highest temperature possible (usually around 500°F or 260°C).
2. On a floured surface, roll out the pizza dough into a round disc, about 10 to 12 inches (25 to 30 cm) in diameter.
3. Transfer the rolled-out dough to a pizza peel or a baking sheet lined with parchment paper.
4. Spread a layer of tomato sauce evenly over the dough, leaving a small border around the edges.
5. Sprinkle an ample amount of mozzarella cheese, crumbled gorgonzola cheese, grated Parmesan cheese, and shredded Fontina cheese over the sauce.
6. Cook the pizza in the preheated oven for approximately 10 to 12 minutes, or until the crust is golden and crispy, and the cheese is melted and nicely browned.
7. Remove the pizza from the oven and let it cool for a few minutes.
8. Slice and serve hot.

PROSCIUTTO E FUNGHI

Dough Recipe
Classic Neapolitan-Style

Ingredients
- Pizza dough (Neapolitan-style), ready to use
- Tomato sauce
- Mozzarella cheese
- Ham, thinly sliced
- Mushrooms, sliced
- Fresh basil leaves (optional)
- Extra-virgin olive oil
- Salt

Nutritional Values
(per pizza, approximate)
- 1000 cal
- Carbohydrates: 100g
- Protein: 40g
- Fat: 45g

Preparation
1. Preheat your oven to the highest temperature possible (usually around 500°F or 260°C).
2. On a floured surface, roll out the pizza dough into a round disc, about 10 to 12 inches (25 to 30 cm) in diameter.
3. Transfer the rolled-out dough to a pizza peel or a baking sheet lined with parchment paper.
4. Spread a layer of tomato sauce evenly over the dough, leaving a small border around the edges.
5. Arrange slices of prosciutto and sliced mushrooms over the sauce.
6. If desired, garnish with fresh basil leaves.
7. Drizzle with a little extra-virgin olive oil and sprinkle with a pinch of salt.
8. Sprinkle an ample amount of mozzarella cheese over the toppings.
9. Cook the pizza in the preheated oven for approximately 10 to 12 minutes, or until the crust is golden and crispy, and the cheese is melted and nicely browned.
10. Remove the pizza from the oven and let it cool for a few minutes.
11. Slice and serve hot.

CACIO E PEPE

Dough Recipe
Classic Neapolitan-Style

Ingredients
- Pizza dough (Neapolitan-style), ready to use
- Extra-virgin olive oil
- Pecorino Romano cheese, grated
- Black pepper, freshly ground
- Fresh parsley, chopped (optional)

Nutritional Values
(per pizza, approximate)
- 900 cal
- Carbohydrates: 115g
- Protein: 35g
- Fat: 40g

Preparation
1. Preheat your oven to the highest temperature possible (usually around 500°F or 260°C).
2. On a floured surface, roll out the pizza dough into a round disc, about 10 to 12 inches (25 to 30 cm) in diameter.
3. Transfer the rolled-out dough to a pizza peel or a baking sheet lined with parchment paper.
4. Drizzle the pizza dough with a generous amount of extra-virgin olive oil.
5. Sprinkle an ample amount of grated Pecorino Romano cheese over the dough, covering the surface evenly.
6. Grind black pepper to taste over the cheese.
7. Bake the pizza in the preheated oven for about 10 to 12 minutes until the crust is golden brown.
8. Remove the pizza from the oven and let it cool for a few minutes.
9. If desired, garnish with freshly chopped parsley.
10. Slice and serve hot.

FRUTTI DI MARE

Dough Recipe
Classic Neapolitan-Style

Ingredients
- Pizza dough (Neapolitan-style), ready to use
- Tomato sauce
- Mozzarella cheese
- Assorted seafood (shrimp, mussels, calamari, etc.)
- Garlic cloves, minced
- Extra-virgin olive oil
- Fresh parsley, chopped
- Lemon wedges (optional)
- Salt
- Red pepper flakes (optional)

Nutritional Values
(per pizza, approximate)
- 1000 cal
- Carbohydrates: 115g
- Protein: 40g
- Fat: 40g

Preparation
1. Preheat your oven to the highest temperature possible (usually around 500°F or 260°C).
2. On a floured surface, roll out the pizza dough into a round disc, about 10 to 12 inches (25 to 30 cm) in diameter.
3. Transfer the rolled-out dough to a pizza peel or a baking sheet lined with parchment paper.
4. Spread a layer of tomato sauce evenly over the dough, leaving a small border around the edges.
5. Sprinkle an ample amount of mozzarella cheese over the sauce.
6. Distribute the assorted seafood over the cheese.
7. In a small bowl, combine minced garlic, extra-virgin olive oil, chopped parsley, salt, and red pepper flakes (if desired).
8. Drizzle the garlic-oil mixture over the pizza toppings.
9. Cook the pizza in the preheated oven for approximately 10 to 12 minutes, or until the crust is golden and crispy, and the cheese is melted and nicely browned.
10. Remove the pizza from the oven and let it cool for a few minutes.
11. If desired, squeeze fresh lemon juice over the pizza before serving.
12. Slice and serve hot.

PATATINE FRITTE

Dough Recipe
Classic Neapolitan-Style

Ingredients

- Pizza dough (Neapolitan-style), ready to use
- Tomato sauce
- Mozzarella cheese
- French fries (precooked)
- Fresh rosemary, chopped
- Salt
- Olive oil

Nutritional Values
(per pizza, approximate)

- 1100 cal
- Carbohydrates: 120g
- Protein: 35g
- Fat: 50g

Preparation

1. Preheat your oven to the highest temperature possible (usually around 500°F or 260°C).
2. On a floured surface, roll out the pizza dough into a round disc, about 10 to 12 inches (25 to 30 cm) in diameter.
3. Transfer the rolled-out dough to a pizza peel or a baking sheet lined with parchment paper.
4. Spread a layer of tomato sauce evenly over the dough, leaving a small border around the edges.
5. Sprinkle an ample amount of mozzarella cheese over the sauce.
6. Distribute the precooked French fries evenly over the cheese.
7. Sprinkle chopped fresh rosemary and a pinch of salt over the pizza.
8. Drizzle a little olive oil over the toppings.
9. Cook the pizza in the preheated oven for approximately 10 to 12 minutes, or until the crust is golden and crispy, and the cheese is melted and nicely browned.
10. Remove the pizza from the oven and let it cool for a few minutes.
11. Slice and serve hot.

ROMANA

Dough Recipe
Classic Neapolitan-Style

Ingredients

- Pizza dough (Neapolitan-Style), ready to use
- Tomato sauce
- Mozzarella cheese
- Anchovies
- Black olives, pitted and halved
- Oregano
- Olive oil

Nutritional Values
(per pizza, approximate)

- 1000 cal
- Carbohydrates: 115g
- Protein: 40g
- Fat: 45g

Preparation

1. Preheat your oven to 475°F (245°C) or the highest temperature possible.
2. On a floured surface, roll out the pizza dough into a rectangular shape, about 14 to 16 inches (35 to 40 cm) long and 10 to 12 inches (25 to 30 cm) wide.
3. Transfer the rolled-out dough to a baking sheet lined with parchment paper.
4. Spread a layer of tomato sauce evenly over the dough, leaving a small border around the edges.
5. Place anchovies and black olives evenly over the sauce.
6. Sprinkle oregano over the toppings.
7. Drizzle a little olive oil over the pizza.
8. Bake the pizza in the preheated oven for about 12 to 15 minutes until the crust is golden brown and crispy.
9. Remove the pizza from the oven and let it cool for a few minutes.
10. Slice and serve hot.

SICILIANA

Dough Recipe
Classic Neapolitan-Style

Ingredients
- Pizza dough (Neapolitan-Style), ready to use
- Tomato sauce
- Mozzarella cheese
- Eggplant, sliced
- Cherry tomatoes, halved
- Black olives, pitted and halved
- Capers
- Fresh basil leaves
- Extra-virgin olive oil
- Salt
- Red pepper flakes (optional)

Nutritional Values
(per pizza, approximate)
- 1100 cal
- Carbohydrates: 120g
- Protein: 40g
- Fat: 45g

Preparation
1. Preheat your oven to 475°F (245°C) or the highest temperature possible.
2. On a floured surface, roll out the pizza dough into a rectangular shape, about 14 to 16 inches (35 to 40 cm) long and 10 to 12 inches (25 to 30 cm) wide.
3. Transfer the rolled-out dough to a baking sheet lined with parchment paper.
4. Spread a layer of tomato sauce evenly over the dough, leaving a small border around the edges.
5. Arrange sliced eggplant, cherry tomatoes, and black olives over the sauce.
6. Sprinkle capers and torn fresh basil leaves over the toppings.
7. Drizzle a little extra-virgin olive oil over the pizza.
8. Season with a pinch of salt and red pepper flakes (if desired).
9. Cook the pizza in the preheated oven for approximately 10 to 12 minutes, or until the crust is golden and crispy, and the cheese is melted and nicely browned.
10. Remove the pizza from the oven and let it cool for a few minutes.
11. Slice and serve hot.

CAPRESE

Dough Recipe
Classic Neapolitan-Style

Ingredients
- Pizza dough (Neapolitan-style), ready to use
- Fresh mozzarella cheese, sliced
- Fresh tomatoes, sliced
- Fresh basil leaves
- Extra-virgin olive oil
- Balsamic glaze (optional)
- Salt
- Black pepper

Nutritional Values
(per pizza, approximate)
- 1000 cal
- Carbohydrates: 115g
- Protein: 35g
- Fat: 40g

Preparation
1. Preheat your oven to the highest temperature possible (usually around 500°F or 260°C).
2. On a floured surface, roll out the pizza dough into a round disc, about 10 to 12 inches (25 to 30 cm) in diameter.
3. Transfer the rolled-out dough to a pizza peel or a baking sheet lined with parchment paper.
4. Arrange slices of fresh mozzarella cheese and tomatoes alternately over the dough.
5. Place fresh basil leaves between the cheese and tomato slices.
6. Drizzle a little extra-virgin olive oil over the toppings.
7. Season with salt and black pepper to taste.
8. Bake the pizza in the preheated oven for about 10 to 12 minutes until the crust is golden brown and the cheese is melted.
9. Remove the pizza from the oven and let it cool for a few minutes.
10. If desired, drizzle balsamic glaze over the pizza before serving.
11. Slice and serve hot.

ORTOLANA

Dough Recipe
Classic Neapolitan-Style

Ingredients
- Pizza dough (Neapolitan-style), ready to use
- Tomato sauce
- Mozzarella cheese
- Assorted vegetables (such as bell peppers, zucchini, eggplant, mushrooms), sliced or diced
- Onion, thinly sliced
- Garlic cloves, minced
- Fresh basil leaves, torn
- Extra-virgin olive oil
- Salt
- Black pepper

Nutritional Values
(per pizza, approximate)
- 1000 cal
- Carbohydrates: 115g
- Protein: 35g
- Fat: 40g

Preparation
1. Preheat your oven to the highest temperature possible (usually around 500°F or 260°C).
2. On a floured surface, roll out the pizza dough into a round disc, about 10 to 12 inches (25 to 30 cm) in diameter.
3. Transfer the rolled-out dough to a pizza peel or a baking sheet lined with parchment paper.
4. Spread a layer of tomato sauce evenly over the dough, leaving a small border around the edges.
5. Sprinkle an ample amount of mozzarella cheese over the sauce.
6. Arrange the assorted vegetables, onion slices, and minced garlic over the cheese.
7. Scatter torn basil leaves over the toppings.
8. Drizzle a little extra-virgin olive oil over the pizza.
9. Season with salt and black pepper to taste.
10. Cook the pizza in the preheated oven for approximately 10 to 12 minutes, or until the crust is golden and crispy, and the cheese is melted and nicely browned.
11. Remove the pizza from the oven and let it cool for a few minutes.
12. Slice and serve hot.

TONNO E CIPOLLA

Dough Recipe
Classic Neapolitan-Style

Ingredients
- Pizza dough (Neapolitan-style), ready to use
- Tomato sauce
- Mozzarella cheese
- Canned tuna, drained
- Red onion, thinly sliced
- Fresh parsley, chopped
- Extra-virgin olive oil
- Salt
- Black pepper

Nutritional Values
(per pizza, approximate)
- 1000 cal
- Carbohydrates: 110g
- Protein: 40g
- Fat: 40g

Preparation
1. Preheat your oven to the highest temperature possible (usually around 500°F or 260°C).
2. On a floured surface, roll out the pizza dough into a round disc, about 10 to 12 inches (25 to 30 cm) in diameter.
3. Transfer the rolled-out dough to a pizza peel or a baking sheet lined with parchment paper.
4. Spread a layer of tomato sauce evenly over the dough, leaving a small border around the edges.
5. Sprinkle an ample amount of mozzarella cheese over the sauce.
6. Distribute the canned tuna and red onion slices over the cheese.
7. Sprinkle chopped fresh parsley over the toppings.
8. Drizzle a little extra-virgin olive oil over the pizza.
9. Season with salt and black pepper to taste.
10. Cook the pizza in the preheated oven for approximately 10 to 12 minutes, or until the crust is golden and crispy, and the cheese is melted and nicely browned.
11. Remove the pizza from the oven and let it cool for a few minutes.
12. Slice and serve hot.

SALSICCIA E FRIARIELLI

Dough Recipe
Classic Neapolitan-Style

Ingredients
- Pizza dough (Neapolitan-style), ready to use
- Tomato sauce
- Mozzarella cheese
- Italian sausage, cooked and sliced
- Broccoli rabe (friarielli), blanched and chopped
- Garlic cloves, minced
- Red pepper flakes
- Extra-virgin olive oil
- Salt
- Black pepper

Nutritional Values
(per pizza, approximate)
- 1100 cal
- Carbohydrates: 110g
- Protein: 45g
- Fat: 45g

Preparation
1. Preheat your oven to the highest temperature possible (usually around 500°F or 260°C).
2. On a floured surface, roll out the pizza dough into a round disc, about 10 to 12 inches (25 to 30 cm) in diameter.
3. Transfer the rolled-out dough to a pizza peel or a baking sheet lined with parchment paper.
4. Spread a layer of tomato sauce evenly over the dough, leaving a small border around the edges.
5. Sprinkle an ample amount of mozzarella cheese over the sauce.
6. Arrange the cooked Italian sausage slices and chopped broccoli rabe over the cheese.
7. Sprinkle minced garlic and red pepper flakes over the toppings.
8. Drizzle a little extra-virgin olive oil over the pizza.
9. Season with salt and black pepper to taste.
10. Bake the pizza in the preheated oven for about 10 to 12 minutes until the crust is golden brown and the cheese is melted and bubbly.
11. Remove the pizza from the oven and let it cool for a few minutes.
12. Slice and serve hot.

CARBONARA

Dough Recipe
Classic Neapolitan-Style

Ingredients
- Pizza dough (Neapolitan-style), ready to use
- Mozzarella cheese
- Pancetta or bacon, cooked and chopped
- 1 Egg
- Pecorino Romano cheese, grated
- Freshly ground black pepper
- Extra-virgin olive oil

Nutritional Values
(per pizza, approximate)
- 1000 cal
- Carbohydrates: 100g
- Protein: 40g
- Fat: 35g

Preparation
1. Preheat your oven to the highest temperature possible (usually around 500°F or 260°C).
2. On a floured surface, roll out the pizza dough into a round disc, about 10 to 12 inches (25 to 30 cm) in diameter.
3. Transfer the rolled-out dough to a pizza peel or a baking sheet lined with parchment paper.
4. Sprinkle an ample amount of mozzarella cheese over the dough.
5. Distribute the cooked pancetta or bacon evenly over the cheese.
6. Create small wells in the toppings and crack the egg into them.
7. Sprinkle grated Pecorino Romano cheese and freshly ground black pepper over the pizza.
8. Drizzle a little extra-virgin olive oil over the toppings.
9. Bake the pizza in the preheated oven for about 10 to 12 minutes until the crust is golden brown and the eggs are cooked to your liking.
10. Remove the pizza from the oven and let it cool for a few minutes.
11. Slice and serve hot.

GORGONZOLA E NOCI

Dough Recipe
Classic Neapolitan-Style

Ingredients
- Pizza dough (Neapolitan-style), ready to use
- Gorgonzola cheese, crumbled
- Mozzarella cheese
- Walnuts, roughly chopped
- Fresh thyme leaves
- Honey
- Extra-virgin olive oil

Nutritional Values
(per pizza, approximate)
- 1000 cal
- Carbohydrates: 100g
- Protein: 35g
- Fat: 50g

Preparation
1. Preheat your oven to the highest temperature possible (usually around 500°F or 260°C).
2. On a floured surface, roll out the pizza dough into a round disc, about 10 to 12 inches (25 to 30 cm) in diameter.
3. Transfer the rolled-out dough to a pizza peel or a baking sheet lined with parchment paper.
4. Sprinkle an ample amount of crumbled gorgonzola cheese over the dough.
5. Add a layer of mozzarella cheese on top of the gorgonzola.
6. Sprinkle the chopped walnuts and fresh thyme leaves evenly over the cheese.
7. Drizzle a little honey over the toppings.
8. Drizzle a little extra-virgin olive oil over the pizza.
9. Cook the pizza in the preheated oven for approximately 10 to 12 minutes, or until the crust is golden and crispy, and the cheese is melted and nicely browned.
10. Remove the pizza from the oven and let it cool for a few minutes.
11. Slice and serve hot.

PATATE E ROSMARINO

Dough Recipe
Classic Neapolitan-Style

Ingredients
- Pizza dough (Neapolitan-style), ready to use
- Thinly-sliced potatoes
- Fresh rosemary leaves
- Mozzarella cheese
- Extra-virgin olive oil
- Salt
- Black pepper

Nutritional Values
(per pizza, approximate)
- 900 cal
- Carbohydrates: 110g
- Protein: 35g
- Fat: 35g

Preparation
1. Preheat your oven to the highest temperature possible (usually around 500°F or 260°C).
2. On a floured surface, roll out the pizza dough into a round disc, about 10 to 12 inches (25 to 30 cm) in diameter.
3. Transfer the rolled-out dough to a pizza peel or a baking sheet lined with parchment paper.
4. Arrange the thinly-sliced potatoes evenly over the dough.
5. Sprinkle fresh rosemary leaves over the potatoes.
6. Sprinkle an ample amount of mozzarella cheese over the toppings.
7. Drizzle a little extra-virgin olive oil over the pizza.
8. Season with salt and black pepper to taste.
9. Cook the pizza in the preheated oven for approximately 10 to 12 minutes, or until the crust is golden and crispy, and the cheese is melted and nicely browned.
10. Remove the pizza from the oven and let it cool for a few minutes.
11. Slice and serve hot.

NEW YORK-STYLE

New York-style pizza is a variety of pizza originating from New York City, which is famous for its thin and crispy crust with thick and fluffy edges. This style of pizza is widely recognized for its large and foldable format, allowing people to eat a slice with their hands while walking the streets of the Big Apple.

The distinctive features of New York-style pizza include a thin and crispy crust at the base of the slice, gradually becoming thicker and softer towards the outer edge. The dough is typically prepared with flour, water, yeast, salt, and olive oil. It is fermented for a shorter period of time compared to other pizza styles, which contributes to its light and crispy texture.

New York-style pizza is often topped with tomato sauce and mozzarella, but it also offers a variety of other topping options such as sausage, pepperoni, mushrooms, onions, and chili. It is then baked in a very hot oven, giving the pizza a characteristic flavor and a crispy crust.

Classic New York-style Dough Recipe

Ingredients for 5 medium-sized pizzas:
- 2.2 lbs type "00" flour (1 kg)
- 2.25 cups water (550 ml)
- 0.25 oz fresh yeast (7 g)
- 0.7 oz salt (20 g)
- 0.25 cup olive oil (60 ml)

Start by dissolving the fresh yeast in room temperature water. In a large bowl, mix the flour and salt, then add the water with the yeast and the olive oil. Mix the ingredients until you obtain a homogeneous dough.

Transfer the dough onto a lightly floured work surface and knead vigorously for about 10 to 15 minutes, until it becomes smooth and elastic. Shape the dough into a ball and place it in a lightly oiled bowl. Cover the bowl with a damp cloth and let the dough rise at room temperature for about 1 to 2 hours, or until it doubles in size.

Once the dough has risen, divide it into 5 uniform-sized balls, usually around 6.3 to 7.1 ounces (180 to 200 grams) each. Roll each of them out on a lightly oiled pizza pan or baking sheet and top them with your favorite ingredients.

CLASSIC CHEESE PIZZA

Dough Recipe
Classic New York-Style

Ingredients
- Pizza dough (New York-style), ready to use
- 1 cup tomato sauce
- 2 cups shredded mozzarella cheese
- Fresh basil leaves
- Olive oil

Preparation
1. Preheat your oven to 475°F (245°C).
2. On a lightly floured surface, roll out the pizza dough into a 12-inch (30 cm) round.
3. Transfer the rolled-out dough to a pizza peel or a baking sheet lined with parchment paper.
4. Spread the tomato sauce evenly over the dough, leaving a small border around the edges.
5. Sprinkle the shredded mozzarella cheese over the sauce.
6. Tear some fresh basil leaves and scatter them on top of the cheese.
7. Drizzle a little olive oil over the pizza.
8. Cook the pizza in the preheated oven for approximately 12 to 15 minutes, or until the crust is golden and crispy, and the cheese is melted and nicely browned.
9. Remove the pizza from the oven and let it cool for a few minutes before slicing.
10. Serve hot and enjoy!

Nutritional Values
(per pizza, approximate)
- 1200 cal
- Carbohydrates: 140g
- Protein: 60g
- Fat: 50g

PEPPERONI PIZZA

Dough Recipe
Classic New York-Style

Ingredients
- Pizza dough (New York-style), ready to use
- 1 cup tomato sauce
- 2 cups shredded mozzarella cheese
- Sliced pepperoni
- Crushed red pepper flakes (optional)

Preparation
1. Preheat the oven to 475°F (245°C).
2. Roll out the pizza dough on a floured surface into a 12-inch (30 cm) round.
3. Transfer the dough to a pizza peel or baking sheet lined with parchment paper.
4. Spread the tomato sauce evenly over the dough.
5. Sprinkle the shredded mozzarella cheese over the sauce.
6. Place the sliced pepperoni on top of the cheese.
7. If desired, sprinkle some crushed red pepper flakes for a spicy kick.
8. Bake the pizza in a preheated oven at 475°F (245°C) for 12 to 15 minutes or until the crust is golden brown and the cheese is melted and bubbly.
9. Allow the pizza to cool slightly before slicing and serving.

Nutritional Values
(per pizza, approximate)
- 1300 cal
- Carbohydrates: 140g
- Protein: 65g
- Fat: 55g

WHITE PIZZA

Dough Recipe
Classic New York-Style

Ingredients
- Pizza dough (New York-style), ready to use
- 2 cloves garlic, minced
- Olive oil
- 1.5 cups shredded mozzarella cheese
- 0.5 cup ricotta cheese
- 0.25 cup grated pecorino cheese
- Fresh parsley, chopped

Nutritional Values
(per pizza, approximate)
- 1150 cal
- Carbohydrates: 120g
- Protein: 55g
- Fat: 50g

Preparation
1. Preheat the oven to 475°F (245°C).
2. Roll out the pizza dough on a floured surface into a 12-inch (30 cm) round.
3. Transfer the dough to a pizza peel or baking sheet lined with parchment paper.
4. In a small bowl, mix the minced garlic with a drizzle of olive oil.
5. Brush the garlic-infused oil evenly over the dough, leaving a small border around the edges.
6. Sprinkle the shredded mozzarella cheese over the oiled dough.
7. Dot the surface with spoonfuls of ricotta cheese.
8. Sprinkle grated pecorino cheese over the top.
9. Drizzle a little more olive oil over the pizza.
10. Cook the pizza in the preheated oven for approximately 12 to 15 minutes, or until the crust is golden and crispy, and the cheese is melted and nicely browned.
11. Remove from the oven and garnish with fresh chopped parsley.
12. Allow the pizza to cool slightly before slicing and serving.

MEAT LOVER'S PIZZA

Dough Recipe
Classic New York-Style

Ingredients
- Pizza dough (New York-style), ready to use
- 1 cup tomato sauce
- 2 cups shredded mozzarella cheese
- Sliced salami
- Sliced bacon
- Sliced Italian sausage
- Sliced ham
- Fresh basil leaves

Nutritional Values
(per pizza, approximate)
- 1500 cal
- Carbohydrates: 140g
- Protein: 80g
- Fat: 75g

Preparation
1. Preheat the oven to 475°F (245°C).
2. Roll out the pizza dough on a floured surface into a 12-inch (30 cm) round.
3. Transfer the dough to a pizza peel or baking sheet lined with parchment paper.
4. Spread the tomato sauce evenly over the dough.
5. Sprinkle the shredded mozzarella cheese over the sauce.
6. Arrange the sliced salami, bacon, Italian sausage, and ham on top of the cheese.
7. Tear some fresh basil leaves and sprinkle them over the toppings.
8. Bake the pizza in a preheated oven at 475°F (245°C) for 12 to 15 minutes or until the crust is golden brown and the cheese is melted and bubbly.
9. Allow the pizza to cool slightly before slicing and serving.

CREAMY DREAM PIZZA

Dough Recipe
Classic New York-Style

Ingredients

- Pizza dough (New York-style), ready to use
- 1 cup shredded mozzarella cheese
- 0.5 cup grated Parmesan cheese
- 0.5 cup white sauce (previously prepared or store-bought)
- 1 cup fresh spinach
- 0.5 cup thinly-sliced red onion
- 2 cloves garlic, minced
- 2 tsp olive oil
- Salt, to taste
- Pepper, to taste

Nutritional Values
(per pizza, approximate)

- 1500 cal
- Carbohydrates: 140g
- Protein: 80g
- Fat: 75g

Preparation

1. Preheat the oven to 475°F (245°C).
2. Roll out the pizza dough on a lightly floured surface to your desired thickness.
3. Transfer the dough to a baking sheet or pizza stone.
4. Spread the white sauce evenly over the dough, leaving a small border around the edges.
5. Sprinkle the shredded mozzarella and grated Parmesan cheese over the white sauce.
6. Distribute the fresh spinach and red onion slices on top of the cheese.
7. In a small skillet, heat the olive oil and minced garlic for a few minutes. Drizzle the garlic-infused olive oil over the pizza.
8. Season with salt and pepper to taste.
9. Cook the pizza in the preheated oven for approximately 12 to 15 minutes, or until the crust is golden and crispy, and the cheese is melted and nicely browned.
10. Remove the pizza from the oven and let it cool for a few minutes before slicing and serving.

BBQ CHICKEN PIZZA

Dough Recipe
Classic New York-Style

Ingredients

- Pizza dough (New York-style), ready to use
- 0.5 cup BBQ sauce
- 2 cups shredded mozzarella cheese
- Cooked chicken breast, shredded
- Red onion, thinly sliced
- Fresh cilantro leaves

Nutritional Values
(per pizza, approximate)

- 1250 cal
- Carbohydrates: 140g
- Protein: 70g
- Fat: 45g

Preparation

1. Preheat the oven to 475°F (245°C).
2. Roll out the pizza dough into a 12-inch (30 cm) round on a floured surface.
3. Transfer the dough to a pizza peel or baking sheet lined with parchment paper.
4. Spread the BBQ sauce evenly over the dough, leaving a small border around the edges.
5. Sprinkle the shredded mozzarella cheese over the sauce.
6. Spread the shredded chicken evenly over the cheese.
7. Top with sliced red onion.
8. Cook the pizza in the preheated oven for approximately 12 to 15 minutes, or until the crust is golden and crispy, and the cheese is melted and nicely browned.
9. Remove from the oven and garnish with fresh cilantro leaves.
10. Allow the pizza to cool slightly before slicing and serving.

BUFFALO CHICKEN PIZZA

Dough Recipe
Classic New York-Style

Ingredients
- Pizza dough (New York-style), ready to use
- 0.5 cup hot sauce
- 2 cups shredded mozzarella cheese
- Cooked chicken breast, shredded
- Ranch dressing
- Red onion, thinly sliced
- Fresh cilantro leaves

Nutritional Values
(per pizza, approximate)
- 1300 cal
- Carbohydrates: 135g
- Protein: 70g
- Fat: 50g

Preparation
1. Preheat the oven to 475°F (245°C).
2. Roll out the pizza dough into a 12-inch (30 cm) round on a floured surface.
3. Transfer the dough to a pizza peel or baking sheet lined with parchment paper.
4. Spread the hot sauce evenly over the dough, leaving a small border around the edges.
5. Sprinkle the shredded mozzarella cheese over the sauce.
6. Spread the shredded chicken evenly over the cheese.
7. Drizzle ranch dressing over the chicken.
8. Top with sliced red onion.
9. Cook the pizza in the preheated oven for approximately 12 to 15 minutes, or until the crust is golden and crispy, and the cheese is melted and nicely browned.
10. Remove from the oven and garnish with fresh cilantro leaves.
11. Allow the pizza to cool slightly before slicing and serving.

TROPICAL TUNA DELIGHT

Dough Recipe
Classic New York-Style

Ingredients
- Pizza dough (New York-style), ready to use
- 0.5 cup pizza sauce
- 1 cup shredded mozzarella cheese
- 0.25 cup canned corn kernels, drained
- 0.25 cup canned tuna, drained
- 0.25 cup sliced black olives
- 1 tbsp olive oil
- 0.5 tsp dried oregano
- Salt, to taste
- Pepper, to taste

Nutritional Values
(per pizza, approximate)
- 1100 cal
- Carbohydrates: 130g
- Protein: 50g
- Fat: 45g

Preparation
1. Preheat the oven to 475°F (245°C).
2. Roll out the pizza dough into a 12-inch (30 cm) round on a floured surface.
3. Transfer the dough to a pizza peel or baking sheet lined with parchment paper.
4. Spread the pizza sauce evenly over the dough, leaving a small border around the edges.
5. Sprinkle the shredded mozzarella cheese over the sauce.
6. Evenly distribute the corn, tuna, and black olive slices on top of the cheese.
7. Drizzle the olive oil over the toppings and sprinkle with dried oregano, salt, and pepper.
8. Cook the pizza in the preheated oven for approximately 12 to 15 minutes, or until the crust is golden and crispy, and the cheese is melted and nicely browned.
9. Remove the pizza from the oven and let it cool for a few minutes before slicing and serving.

VEGGIE DELIGHT PIZZA

Dough Recipe
Classic New York-Style

Ingredients

- Pizza dough (New York-style), ready to use
- 1 cup tomato sauce
- 2 cups shredded mozzarella cheese
- Green bell peppers, thinly sliced
- Cherry tomatoes, halved
- Sliced mushrooms
- Red onion, thinly sliced
- Sliced black olives
- Fresh basil leaves

Nutritional Values
(per pizza, approximate)
- 1100 cal
- Carbohydrates: 130g
- Protein: 50g
- Fat: 45g

Preparation

1. Preheat the oven to 475°F (245°C).
2. Roll out the pizza dough into a 12-inch (30 cm) round on a floured surface.
3. Transfer the dough to a pizza peel or baking sheet lined with parchment paper.
4. Spread the tomato sauce evenly over the dough, leaving a small border around the edges.
5. Sprinkle the shredded mozzarella cheese over the sauce.
6. Arrange the sliced green bell peppers, cherry tomatoes, mushrooms, red onion, and black olives on top of the cheese.
7. Tear some fresh basil leaves and sprinkle them over the toppings.
8. Cook the pizza in the preheated oven for approximately 12 to 15 minutes, or until the crust is golden and crispy, and the cheese is melted and nicely browned.
9. Allow the pizza to cool slightly before slicing and serving.

TOFU TEMPTATION PIZZA

Dough Recipe
Classic New York-Style

Ingredients

- Pizza dough (New York-style), ready to use
- 0.5 cup pizza sauce
- 1 cup crumbled tofu-based vegan cheese
- 0.5 cup extra-firm tofu, diced
- 0.25 cup sliced black olives
- 0.25 cup thinly sliced red onion
- 0.25 cup sliced bell peppers
- 1 tbsp olive oil
- 0.5 tsp dried oregano
- Salt, to taste
- Pepper, to taste

Nutritional Values
(per pizza, approximate)
- 1100 cal
- Carbohydrates: 130g
- Protein: 50g
- Fat: 45g

Preparation

1. Preheat the oven to 475°F (245°C).
2. Roll out the pizza dough into a 12-inch (30 cm) round on a floured surface.
3. Spread the pizza sauce evenly over the dough, leaving a small border around the edges.
4. Sprinkle the crumbled tofu-based vegan cheese over the sauce.
5. Evenly distribute the diced tofu, black olives, red onion, and bell peppers on top of the pizza.
6. Drizzle with olive oil, sprinkle with dried oregano, salt, and pepper.
7. Cook the pizza in the preheated oven for approximately 12 to 15 minutes, or until the crust is golden and crispy, and the cheese is melted and nicely browned.
8. Remove the pizza from the oven and let it cool for a few minutes before slicing and serving.

WHITE CLAM PIZZA

Dough Recipe
Classic New York-Style

Ingredients

- Pizza dough (New York-style), ready to use
- 2 cloves garlic, minced
- Olive oil
- 2 cups shredded mozzarella cheese
- Fresh clams, shucked
- Fresh parsley, chopped

Nutritional Values
(per pizza, approximate)

- 1050 cal
- Carbohydrates: 100g
- Protein: 60g
- Fat: 40g

Preparation

1. Preheat the oven to 475°F (245°C).
2. Roll out the pizza dough into a 12-inch (30 cm) round on a floured surface.
3. Transfer the dough to a pizza peel or baking sheet lined with parchment paper.
4. In a small bowl, mix the minced garlic with a drizzle of olive oil.
5. Spread the garlic and oil mixture evenly over the dough, leaving a small border around the edges.
6. Sprinkle the shredded mozzarella cheese over the garlic.
7. Distribute the fresh clams evenly over the cheese.
8. Drizzle a little more olive oil over the clams.
9. Cook the pizza in the preheated oven for approximately 12 to 15 minutes, or until the crust is golden and crispy, and the cheese is melted and nicely browned.
10. Remove from the oven and sprinkle fresh parsley over the pizza.
11. Allow the pizza to cool slightly before slicing and serving.

MAMMA MIA MEXICANA PIZZA

Dough Recipe
Classic New York-Style

Ingredients

- Pizza dough (New York-style), ready to use
- 0.5 cup pizza sauce
- 1 cup shredded mozzarella cheese
- 0.25 cup canned corn kernels
- 0.25 cup sliced bell peppers (any color you prefer)
- 0.25 cup sliced pepperoni
- 1 tbsp olive oil
- 0.5 tsp dried oregano
- Salt, to taste
- Pepper, to taste

Nutritional Values
(per pizza, approximate)

- 950 cal
- Carbohydrates: 110g
- Protein: 50g
- Fat: 40g

Preparation

1. Preheat the oven to 475°F (245°C).
2. Roll out the pizza dough into a 12-inch (30 cm) round on a floured surface.
3. Transfer the dough to a pizza peel or baking sheet lined with parchment paper.
4. Spread the pizza sauce evenly over the dough, leaving a small border around the edges.
5. Sprinkle the shredded mozzarella cheese over the sauce.
6. Evenly distribute the corn, bell peppers, and pepperoni slices on top of the cheese.
7. Drizzle the olive oil over the toppings and sprinkle with dried oregano, salt, and pepper.
8. Cook the pizza in the preheated oven for approximately 12 to 15 minutes, or until the crust is golden and crispy, and the cheese is melted and nicely browned.
9. Remove the pizza from the oven and let it cool for a few minutes before slicing and serving.

SUPREME PIZZA

Dough Recipe

Classic New York-Style

Ingredients

- Pizza dough (New York-style), ready to use
- 1 cup tomato sauce
- 2 cups shredded mozzarella cheese
- Sliced pepperoni
- Sliced green bell peppers
- Sliced red onions
- Sliced black olives
- Sliced mushrooms

Preparation

1. Preheat the oven to 475°F (245°C).
2. Roll out the pizza dough into a 12-inch (30 cm) round on a floured surface.
3. Transfer the dough to a pizza peel or baking sheet lined with parchment paper.
4. Spread the tomato sauce evenly over the dough, leaving a small border around the edges.
5. Sprinkle the shredded mozzarella cheese over the sauce.
6. Arrange the pepperoni, bell peppers, red onions, black olives, and mushrooms on top of the cheese.
7. Cook the pizza in the preheated oven for approximately 12 to 15 minutes, or until the crust is golden and crispy, and the cheese is melted and nicely browned.
8. Allow the pizza to cool slightly before slicing and serving.

Nutritional Values
(per pizza, approximate)

- 1100 cal
- Carbohydrates: 120g
- Protein: 55g
- Fat: 45g

SPINACH AND FETA PIZZA

Dough Recipe

New York-Style

Ingredients

- Pizza dough (New York-style), ready to use
- Olive oil
- Garlic, minced
- Fresh spinach leaves
- Crumbled feta cheese
- Salt, to taste
- Pepper, to taste

Preparation

1. Preheat the oven to 475°F (245°C).
2. Roll out the pizza dough into a 12-inch (30 cm) round on a floured surface.
3. Transfer the dough to a pizza peel or baking sheet lined with parchment paper.
4. Drizzle olive oil over the dough and spread minced garlic evenly.
5. Arrange fresh spinach leaves over the dough.
6. Sprinkle crumbled feta cheese over the spinach.
7. Season with salt and pepper to taste.
8. Bake for 12 to 15 minutes or until the crust is golden brown and the cheese is melted.
9. Remove from the oven, let it cool slightly, then slice and serve.

Nutritional Values
(per pizza, approximate)

- 880 cal
- Carbohydrates: 97g
- Protein: 36g
- Fat: 40g

PESTO AND CHERRY TOMATO PIZZA

Dough Recipe
New York-Style

Ingredients
- Pizza dough (New York-style), ready to use
- Pesto sauce
- Fresh mozzarella cheese, sliced
- Cherry tomatoes, halved
- Fresh basil leaves
- Salt, to taste
- Pepper, to taste

Preparation
1. Preheat the oven to 475°F (245°C).
2. Roll out the pizza dough into a 12-inch (30 cm) round on a floured surface.
3. Transfer the dough to a pizza peel or baking sheet lined with parchment paper.
4. Spread a thin layer of pesto sauce evenly over the dough.
5. Arrange slices of fresh mozzarella cheese over the pesto.
6. Place halved cherry tomatoes on top.
7. Season with salt and pepper to taste.
8. Bake for 12-15 minutes or until the crust is golden brown and the cheese is melted.
9. Remove from the oven, garnish with fresh basil leaves, let it cool slightly, then slice and serve.

Nutritional Values
(per pizza, approximate)
- 910 cal
- Carbohydrates: 85g
- Protein: 36g
- Fat: 52g

HAWAIIAN PIZZA

Dough Recipe
New York-Style

Ingredients
- Pizza dough (New York-style), ready to use
- Tomato sauce
- Shredded mozzarella cheese
- Sliced ham
- Pineapple chunks

Preparation
1. Preheat the oven to 475°F (245°C).
2. Roll out the pizza dough into a 12-inch (30 cm) round on a floured surface.
3. Transfer the dough to a pizza peel or baking sheet lined with parchment paper.
4. Spread a thin layer of tomato sauce evenly over the dough.
5. Sprinkle shredded mozzarella cheese over the sauce.
6. Arrange sliced ham and pineapple chunks on top.
7. Bake for 12 to 15 minutes or until the crust is golden brown and the cheese is melted.
8. Remove from the oven, let it cool slightly, then slice and serve.

Nutritional Values
(per pizza, approximate)
- 920 cal
- Carbohydrates: 98g
- Protein: 50g
- Fat: 36g

SOUTHWESTERN BEAN DELIGHT

Dough Recipe
New York-Style

Ingredients
- Pizza dough (New York-style), ready to use
- 0.5 cup pizza sauce
- 1 cup shredded mozzarella cheese
- 0.5 cup canned red beans, drained and rinsed
- 0.25 cup canned corn kernels, drained
- 0.25 cup thinly sliced red onion
- 2 or 3 slices of cooked and crumbled bacon (optional)
- 1 tbsp olive oil
- 0.5 tsp dried oregano
- Red pepper flakes (optional)
- Salt, to taste
- Pepper, to taste

Nutritional Values
(per pizza, approximate)
- 950 cal
- Carbohydrates: 80g
- Protein: 45g
- Fat: 52g

Preparation
1. Preheat the oven to 475°F (245°C).
2. Roll out the pizza dough into a 12-inch (30 cm) round on a floured surface.
3. Transfer the dough to a pizza peel or baking sheet lined with parchment paper.
4. Spread the pizza sauce evenly over the dough, leaving a small border around the edges.
5. Sprinkle the shredded mozzarella cheese over the sauce.
6. Evenly distribute the red beans, corn, red onion, and crumbled bacon (if using) on top of the cheese.
7. Drizzle with olive oil, sprinkle with dried oregano, red pepper flakes (if desired, for a spicy kick), salt, and pepper.
8. Bake for 12 to 15 minutes or until the crust is golden brown and the cheese is melted.
9. Remove the pizza from the oven and let it cool for a few minutes before slicing and serving.

SAUSAGE AND PEPPERS PIZZA

Dough Recipe
New York-Style

Ingredients
- Pizza dough (New York-style), ready to use
- Olive oil
- Italian sausage, cooked and sliced
- Sliced bell peppers (red, green, and yellow)
- Sliced onions
- Shredded mozzarella cheese

Nutritional Values
(per pizza, approximate)
- 950 cal
- Carbohydrates: 80g
- Protein: 45g
- Fat: 52g

Preparation
1. Preheat the oven to 475°F (245°C).
2. Roll out the pizza dough into a 12-inch (30 cm) round on a floured surface.
3. Transfer the dough to a pizza peel or baking sheet lined with parchment paper.
4. Drizzle olive oil over the dough.
5. Arrange cooked and sliced Italian sausage on top.
6. Spread sliced bell peppers and onions evenly.
7. Sprinkle shredded mozzarella cheese over the toppings.
8. Cook the pizza in the preheated oven for approximately 12 to 15 minutes, or until the crust is golden and crispy, and the cheese is melted and nicely browned.
9. Remove from the oven, let it cool slightly, then slice and serve.

WHITE PIZZA WITH POTATOES

Dough Recipe
New York-Style

Ingredients
- Pizza dough (New York-style), ready to use
- Olive oil
- Garlic, minced
- Thinly-sliced potatoes
- Fresh rosemary leaves
- Shredded mozzarella cheese
- Salt, to taste
- Pepper, to taste

Preparation
1. Preheat the oven to 475°F (245°C).
2. Roll out the pizza dough into a 12-inch (30 cm) round on a floured surface.
3. Transfer the dough to a pizza peel or baking sheet lined with parchment paper.
4. Drizzle olive oil over the dough and spread minced garlic evenly.
5. Arrange thinly-sliced potatoes over the dough.
6. Sprinkle fresh rosemary leaves and shredded mozzarella cheese over the potatoes.
7. Season with salt and pepper to taste.
8. Bake for 12-15 minutes or until the crust is golden brown and the cheese is melted.
9. Remove from the oven, let it cool slightly, then slice and serve.

Nutritional Values
(per pizza, approximate)
- 880 cal
- Carbohydrates: 97g
- Protein: 36g
- Fat: 40g

GREEK FIESTA PIZZA

Dough Recipe
New York-Style

Ingredients
- Pizza dough (New York-style), ready to use
- 0.5 cup pizza sauce
- 1 cup crumbled feta cheese
- 0.25 cup sun-dried tomatoes, drained and chopped
- 0.25 cup thinly sliced red onion
- 2 tbsp capers, rinsed and drained
- 1 tbsp olive oil
- 0.5 tsp dried oregano
- Salt, to taste
- Pepper, to taste

Preparation
1. Preheat the oven to 475°F (245°C).
2. Roll out the pizza dough on a lightly floured surface to your desired thickness.
3. Transfer the dough to a baking sheet or pizza stone.
4. Spread the pizza sauce evenly over the dough, leaving a small border around the edges.
5. Sprinkle the crumbled feta cheese over the sauce.
6. Distribute the chopped sun-dried tomatoes, thinly sliced red onion, and capers on top of the cheese.
7. Drizzle with olive oil, sprinkle with dried oregano, salt, and pepper.
8. Cook the pizza in the preheated oven for approximately 12 to 15 minutes, or until the crust is golden and crispy, and the cheese is melted and nicely browned.
9. Remove the pizza from the oven and let it cool for a few minutes before slicing and serving.

Nutritional Values
(per pizza, approximate)
- 880 cal
- Carbohydrates: 97g
- Protein: 36g
- Fat: 40g

CHICAGO-STYLE - DEEP-DISH PIZZA

Chicago-Style - Deep-Dish Pizza is an icon of Chicago cuisine in the United States, and even though it doesn't resemble a classic pizza, even the most traditionalists will be won over by it.

Deep-dish pizza is distinguished by its unique characteristics:
- **Thick crust:** The crust of Chicago-style pizza is very thick and tall, creating a sort of "pizza pie" that provides a solid and substantial base for the filling.

- **Cheese layer:** In Chicago-style pizza, the cheese is placed on the dough before the filling. This creates a generous layer of melted cheese that covers the dough, helping to keep it soft, and imparting a rich flavor.

- **Generous filling:** Chicago-style pizza is famous for its filling. It is stuffed with a generous amount of ingredients such as meat, vegetables, cheese, and sauce. This makes the pizza very hearty and flavorful.

- **Tomato sauce:** The tomato sauce is placed on top of the filling, creating a final layer that contributes to the flavor and moisture of the pizza. The sauce can be sweet or have a more robust flavor, depending on preferences.

- **Longer cooking times:** Due to the thick crust and abundance of ingredients, Chicago-style pizza requires longer cooking times compared to other pizza styles. It is usually baked in deep ovens or special pans to ensure that the crust is golden and crispy.

Chicago-Style - Deep-Dish Pizza is an ideal choice for those who love robust pizzas, full of flavor, and with a unique texture.

Chicago-Style - Deep-Dish Dough Recipe

Ingredients to make 2 pizzas:
- 8.8 oz bread flour (250 g)
- 2.3 oz cornmeal (65 g)
- 1 tsp dry yeast
- 1 tsp granulated sugar
- 4.7 fl oz warm water (140 ml)
- 1 tsp salt
- 0.5 oz melted butter (15 g)
- 1 tbsp extra-virgin olive oil

In a bowl, combine the warm water, dry yeast, and granulated sugar. Stir well until the ingredients dissolve, and let it rest for 5 minutes.

In another bowl, mix the bread flour and cornmeal thoroughly with a spoon. Gradually add the water mixture, melted butter, and finally the salt. Knead the dough until it becomes smooth and homogeneous. Shape it into a ball and place it in a bowl. Grease the dough well with olive oil and let it rise for 60 minutes, covering the bowl with plastic wrap. If you want to speed up the process, you can place the bowl in the oven with only the light turned on.

Once the dough has risen, roll it out and line a greased 22-inch diameter pan. The dough should cover the edges of the pan. At this point, you can proceed with the toppings. Chicago-style pizza requires a longer baking time, approximately 20-25 minutes.

CLASSIC CHICAGO-STYLE PIZZA

Dough Recipe
Chicago-Style

Ingredients

- Pizza dough (Chicago-style), ready to use
- 1.5 cups shredded mozzarella cheese
- 1 cup pizza sauce
- 1 cup cooked Italian sausage, crumbled
- 0.5 cup sliced green bell peppers
- 0.5 cup sliced onions
- 0.5 cup sliced mushrooms
- Grated Parmesan cheese (for sprinkling)

Nutritional Values
(per pizza, approximate)
- 2000 cal
- Fat: 100g
- Carbohydrates: 160g
- Protein: 112g

Preparation
1. Preheat the oven to 425°F (220°C). Grease a deep-dish pizza pan with olive oil.
2. Roll out the Chicago-style pizza dough and press it into the prepared pan, covering the bottom and sides evenly. Let it rest for 10 to 15 minutes.
3. Layer the shredded mozzarella cheese evenly over the dough.
4. Spread the pizza sauce over the cheese layer.
5. Add the cooked Italian sausage, sliced green bell peppers, onions, and mushrooms as desired.
6. Sprinkle grated Parmesan cheese on top.
7. Cook the pizza in the oven that has been preheated for approximately 25 to 30 minutes until the crust is golden brown.
8. Remove the pizza from the oven and let it cool for a few minutes before slicing and serving.

DEEP-DISH MARGHERITA PIZZA

Dough Recipe
Chicago-Style

Ingredients

- Pizza dough (Chicago-style), ready to use- Fresh sliced tomatoes
- Buffalo mozzarella, sliced
- Fresh basil leaves
- Olive oil
- Salt and pepper to taste

Nutritional Values
(per pizza, approximate)
- 1500 cal
- Fat: 70g
- Carbohydrates: 160g
- Protein: 70g

Preparation
1. Preheat the oven to 425°F (220°C). Grease a deep-dish pizza pan with olive oil.
2. Roll out the Chicago-style pizza dough and press it into the prepared pan, covering the bottom and sides evenly. Let it rest for 10 to 15 minutes.
3. Layer the sliced buffalo mozzarella evenly on the dough.
4. Add the sliced tomatoes on top of the mozzarella.
5. Sprinkle fresh basil leaves over the tomatoes.
6. Drizzle olive oil over the ingredients and season with salt and pepper.
7. Pour the tomato sauce over the toppings, covering them completely.
8. Cook the pizza in the oven that has been preheated for approximately 25 to 30 minutes until the crust is golden brown.
9. Remove the pizza from the oven and let it cool for a few minutes before slicing and serving.

DEEP-DISH PEPPERONI PIZZA

Dough Recipe
Chicago-Style

Ingredients
- Pizza dough (Chicago-style), ready to use
- Shredded mozzarella cheese
- Pepperoni slices
- Tomato sauce
- Grated Parmesan cheese
- Salt and pepper to taste

Nutritional Values
(per pizza, approximate)
- 1800 cal
- Fat: 80g
- Carbohydrates: 120g
- Protein: 90g

Preparation
1. Preheat the oven to 425°F (220°C). Grease a deep-dish pizza pan with olive oil.
2. Roll out the Chicago-style pizza dough and press it into the prepared pan, covering the bottom and sides evenly. Let it rest for 10 to 15 minutes.
3. Spread a layer of shredded mozzarella cheese on the dough.
4. Arrange pepperoni slices evenly over the cheese.
5. Pour the tomato sauce over the pepperoni, covering them completely.
6. Sprinkle grated Parmesan cheese over the tomato sauce.
7. Season with salt and pepper.
8. Cook the pizza in the oven that has been preheated for approximately 25 to 30 minutes until the crust is golden brown.
9. Remove the pizza from the oven and let it cool for a few minutes before slicing and serving.

DEEP-DISH BBQ CHICKEN PIZZA

Dough Recipe
Chicago-Style

Ingredients
- Pizza dough (Chicago-style), ready to use
- Cooked chicken breast, shredded or diced
- BBQ sauce
- Shredded mozzarella cheese
- Red onion, thinly sliced
- Chopped fresh cilantro
- Salt and pepper to taste

Nutritional Values
(per pizza, approximate)
- 2400 cal
- Fat: 120g
- Carbohydrates: 170g
- Protein: 140g

Preparation
1. Preheat the oven to 425°F (220°C). Grease a deep-dish pizza pan with olive oil.
2. Roll out the Chicago-style pizza dough and press it into the prepared pan, covering the bottom and sides evenly. Let it rest for 10 to 15 minutes.
3. Spread a layer of cooked chicken breast over the dough.
4. Drizzle BBQ sauce over the chicken, covering it completely.
5. Sprinkle a generous amount of shredded mozzarella cheese over the sauce.
6. Top with thinly sliced red onion.
7. Season with salt and pepper.
8. Cook the pizza in the oven that has been preheated for approximately 25 to 30 minutes until the crust is golden brown.
9. Remove the pizza from the oven and sprinkle chopped fresh cilantro on top.
10. Let it cool for a few minutes before slicing and serving.

DEEP-DISH VEGGIE DELIGHT PIZZA

Dough Recipe
Chicago-Style

Ingredients

- Pizza dough (Chicago-style), ready to use
- Tomato sauce
- Shredded mozzarella cheese
- Sliced mushrooms
- Sliced bell peppers
- Sliced onions
- Sliced black olives
- Fresh spinach leaves
- Salt, to taste
- Pepper to taste

Nutritional Values
(per pizza, approximate)

- 2300 cal
- Fat: 100g
- Carbohydrates: 180g
- Protein: 120g

Preparation

1. Preheat the oven to 425°F (220°C). Grease a deep-dish pizza pan with olive oil.
2. Roll out the Chicago-style pizza dough and press it into the prepared pan, covering the bottom and sides evenly. Let it rest for 10 to 15 minutes.
3. Spread a layer of tomato sauce over the dough.
4. Sprinkle a generous amount of shredded mozzarella cheese over the sauce.
5. Layer the sliced mushrooms, bell peppers, onions, black olives, and fresh spinach leaves on top of the cheese.
6. Season with salt and pepper.
7. Cook the pizza in the oven that has been preheated for approximately 25 to 30 minutes until the crust is golden brown.
8. Remove the pizza from the oven and let it cool for a few minutes before slicing and serving.

DEEP-DISH CAPRESE PIZZA

Dough Recipe
Chicago-Style

Ingredients

- Pizza dough (Chicago-style), ready to use
- Fresh sliced tomatoes
- Buffalo mozzarella, sliced
- Fresh basil leaves
- Balsamic glaze
- Salt and pepper to taste

Preparation

1. Preheat the oven to 425°F (220°C). Grease a deep-dish pizza pan with olive oil.
2. Roll out the Chicago-style pizza dough and press it into the prepared pan, covering the bottom and sides evenly. Let it rest for 10 to 15 minutes.
3. Layer the sliced buffalo mozzarella evenly on the dough.
4. Add the sliced tomatoes on top of the mozzarella.
5. Sprinkle fresh basil leaves over the tomatoes.
6. Drizzle balsamic glaze over the ingredients.
7. Season with salt and pepper. Cook the pizza in the oven that has been preheated for approximately 25 to 30 minutes until the crust is golden brown.
8. Remove the pizza from the oven and let it cool for a few minutes before slicing and serving.

Nutritional Values
(per pizza, approximate)

- 2100 cal
- Fat: 100g
- Carbohydrates: 180g
- Protein: 100g

DEEP-DISH HAWAIIAN PIZZA

Dough Recipe
Chicago-Style

Ingredients

- Pizza dough (Chicago-style), ready to use
- Tomato sauce
- Shredded mozzarella cheese
- Sliced ham
- Pineapple chunks
- Shredded coconut
- Salt, to taste
- Pepper, to taste

Nutritional Values
(per pizza, approximate)

- 2200 cal
- Fat: 110g
- Carbohydrates: 180g
- Protein: 120g

Preparation

1. Preheat the oven to 425°F (220°C). Grease a deep-dish pizza pan with olive oil.
2. Roll out the Chicago-style pizza dough and press it into the prepared pan, covering the bottom and sides evenly. Let it rest for 10 to 15 minutes.
3. Spread a layer of tomato sauce over the dough.
4. Sprinkle a generous amount of shredded mozzarella cheese over the sauce.
5. Layer the sliced ham and pineapple chunks on top of the cheese.
6. Sprinkle shredded coconut over the ingredients.
7. Season with salt and pepper.
8. Cook the pizza in the oven that has been preheated for approximately 25 to 30 minutes until the crust is golden brown. Remove the pizza from the oven and let it cool for a few minutes before slicing and serving.

DEEP-DISH SUPREME CHEESY PIZZA

Dough Recipe
Chicago-Style

Ingredients

- Pizza dough (Chicago-style), ready to use
- Tomato sauce
- Shredded mozzarella cheese
- Provolone cheese, sliced
- Gorgonzola cheese, crumbled
- Goat cheese, crumbled
- Salt and pepper to taste

Nutritional Values
(per pizza, approximate)

- 2300 cal
- Fat: 140g
- Carbohydrates: 160g
- Protein: 130g

Preparation

1. Preheat the oven to 425°F (220°C). Grease a deep-dish pizza pan with olive oil.
2. Roll out the Chicago-style pizza dough and press it into the prepared pan, covering the bottom and sides evenly. Let it rest for 10 to 15 minutes.
3. Spread a layer of tomato sauce over the dough.
4. Sprinkle a generous amount of shredded mozzarella cheese over the sauce.
5. Layer the provolone cheese, gorgonzola cheese, and goat cheese on top of the mozzarella.
6. Season with salt and pepper.
7. Cook the pizza in the oven that has been preheated for approximately 25 to 30 minutes until the crust is golden brown.
8. Remove the pizza from the oven and let it cool for a few minutes before slicing and serving.

DEEP-DISH CHICKEN ALFREDO PIZZA

Dough Recipe
Chicago-Style

Ingredients

- Pizza dough (Chicago-style), ready to use
- Grilled chicken breast, sliced
- Alfredo sauce
- Shredded mozzarella cheese
- Fresh spinach leaves
- Caramelized onions
- Salt, to taste
- Pepper, to taste

Nutritional Values
(per pizza, approximate)

- 2500 cal
- Fat: 140g
- Carbohydrates: 170g
- Protein: 150g

Preparation

1. Preheat the oven to 425°F (220°C). Grease a deep-dish pizza pan with olive oil.
2. Roll out the Chicago-style pizza dough and press it into the prepared pan, covering the bottom and sides evenly. Let it rest for 10 to 15 minutes.
3. Spread a layer of Alfredo sauce over the dough.
4. Sprinkle a generous amount of shredded mozzarella cheese over the sauce.
5. Layer the sliced grilled chicken breast, fresh spinach leaves, and caramelized onions on top of the cheese.
6. Season with salt and pepper.
7. Cook the pizza in the oven that has been preheated for approximately 25 to 30 minutes until the crust is golden brown.
8. Remove the pizza from the oven and let it cool for a few minutes before slicing and serving.

DEEP-DISH MEDITERRANEAN PIZZA

Dough Recipe
Chicago-Style

Ingredients

- Pizza dough (Chicago-style), ready to use
- Tomato sauce
- Shredded mozzarella cheese
- Sliced black olives
- Cherry tomatoes, halved
- Sliced red onions
- Pepperoncini peppers, sliced
- Crumbled feta cheese
- Dried oregano
- Salt, to taste
- Pepper, to taste

Nutritional Values
(per pizza, approximate)

- 2200 cal
- Fat: 100g
- Carbohydrates: 170g
- Protein: 120g

Preparation

1. Preheat the oven to 425°F (220°C). Grease a deep-dish pizza pan with olive oil.
2. Roll out the Chicago-style pizza dough and press it into the prepared pan, covering the bottom and sides evenly. Let it rest for 10 to 15 minutes.
3. Spread a layer of tomato sauce over the dough.
4. Sprinkle a generous amount of shredded mozzarella cheese over the sauce.
5. Layer the sliced black olives, cherry tomatoes, red onions, and pepperoncini peppers on top of the cheese.
6. Sprinkle crumbled feta cheese and dried oregano over the ingredients.
7. Season with salt and pepper.
8. Cook the pizza in the oven that has been preheated for approximately 25 to 30 minutes until the crust is golden brown.
9. Remove the pizza from the oven and let it cool for a few minutes before slicing and serving.

DEEP-DISH TACO PIZZA

Dough Recipe
Chicago-Style

Ingredients

- Pizza dough (Chicago-style), ready to use - Ground beef, cooked and seasoned with taco seasoning
- Refried beans
- Shredded cheddar cheese
- Diced tomatoes
- Diced red onions
- Shredded lettuce
- Sliced jalapenos
- Sour cream
- Salt, to taste
- Pepper, to taste

Nutritional Values
(per pizza, approximate)

- 2400 cal
- Fat: 130g
- Carbohydrates: 170g
- Protein: 140g

Preparation

1. Preheat the oven to 425°F (220°C). Grease a deep-dish pizza pan with olive oil.
2. Roll out the Chicago-style pizza dough and press it into the prepared pan, covering the bottom and sides evenly. Let it rest for 10 to 15 minutes.
3. Spread a layer of refried beans over the dough.
4. Sprinkle a generous amount of shredded cheddar cheese over the beans.
5. Spread the cooked and seasoned ground beef evenly over the cheese.
6. Add diced tomatoes, red onions, shredded lettuce, and sliced jalapenos on top of the ground beef.
7. Season with salt and pepper.
8. Cook the pizza in the oven that has been preheated for approximately 25 to 30 minutes until the crust is golden brown.
9. Remove the pizza from the oven and let it cool for a few minutes before slicing and serving.
10. Serve with dollops of sour cream.

DEEP-DISH BBQ BACON CHEESEBURGER PIZZA

Dough Recipe
Chicago-Style

Ingredients

- Pizza dough (Chicago-style), ready to use
- 1 lb (450g) ground beef
- 0.5 cup diced onions
- 0.5 cup diced pickles
- 1 cup shredded mozzarella cheese
- 0.5 cup cheddar cheese, grated
- 0.25 cup BBQ sauce
- 4 slices bacon, cooked and crumbled
- Salt, to taste
- Pepper, to taste

Nutritional Values
(per pizza, approximate)

- 2000 cal
- Fat: 100g
- Carbohydrates: 160g
- Protein: 112g

Preparation

1. Preheat the oven to 425°F (220°C). Grease a deep-dish pizza pan with olive oil.
2. Roll out the Chicago-style pizza dough and press it into the prepared pan, covering the bottom and sides evenly. Let it rest for 10 to 15 minutes.
3. In a skillet, cook the ground beef over medium heat until browned. Add the diced onions, pickles, salt, and pepper. Cook until the onions are translucent and the beef is fully cooked. Drain any excess fat.
4. Spread half of the shredded mozzarella cheese on the bottom of the pizza crust. Layer the cooked ground beef mixture evenly over the cheese.
5. Drizzle the BBQ sauce over the ground beef, then sprinkle the remaining mozzarella cheese and grated cheddar cheese on top. Finally, sprinkle the crumbled bacon over the cheese.
6. Cook the pizza in the oven that has been preheated for approximately 25 to 30 minutes until the crust is golden brown.
7. Remove the pizza from the oven and let it cool for a few minutes before slicing and serving.
8. Enjoy the delicious Deep-Dish BBQ Bacon Cheeseburger pizza!

DEEP-DISH MEAT LOVERS PIZZA

Dough Recipe
Chicago-Style

Ingredients
- Pizza dough (Chicago-style), ready to use
- Tomato sauce
- Shredded mozzarella cheese
- Sliced salami
- Sliced sausage
- Sliced bacon
- Sliced pepperoni

Preparation
1. Preheat the oven to 425°F (220°C). Grease a deep-dish pizza pan with olive oil.
2. Roll out the Chicago pizza dough and press it into the prepared pan, covering the bottom and sides evenly. Let it rest for 10 to 15 minutes.
3. Spread tomato sauce evenly on the dough, leaving a small border around the edges.
4. Sprinkle a generous amount of shredded mozzarella cheese over the sauce.
5. Layer the salami, sausage, bacon, and pepperoni slices on top of the cheese.
6. Cook the pizza in the oven that has been preheated for approximately 25 to 30 minutes until the crust is golden brown.
7. Remove the pizza from the oven and let it cool for a few minutes before slicing and serving.

Nutritional Values
(per pizza, approximate)
- 2400 cal
- Fat: 140g
- Carbohydrates: 180g
- Protein: 120g

DEEP-DISH BUFFALO CHICKEN PIZZA

Dough Recipe
Chicago-Style

Ingredients
- Pizza dough (Chicago-style), ready to use
- Cooked and shredded chicken
- Buffalo sauce
- Shredded mozzarella cheese
- Sliced red onions
- Sliced celery
- Blue cheese crumbles

Preparation
1. Preheat the oven to 425°F (220°C). Grease a deep-dish pizza pan with olive oil.
2. Roll out the Chicago pizza dough and press it into the prepared pan, covering the bottom and sides evenly. Let it rest for 10 to 15 minutes.
3. In a bowl, mix the shredded chicken with buffalo sauce until well coated.
4. Spread a layer of buffalo sauce evenly on the dough.
5. Sprinkle a generous amount of shredded mozzarella cheese over the sauce.
6. Spread the buffalo chicken mixture over the cheese.
7. Top with sliced red onions, celery, and blue cheese crumbles.
8. Cook the pizza in the oven that has been preheated for approximately 25 to 30 minutes until the crust is golden brown.
9. Remove the pizza from the oven and let it cool for a few minutes before slicing and serving.

Nutritional Values
(per pizza, approximate)
- 2200 cal
- Fat: 120g
- Carbohydrates: 160g
- Protein: 120g

DEEP-DISH SPINACH AND ARTICHOKE PIZZA

Dough Recipe
Chicago-Style

Ingredients

- Pizza dough (Chicago-style), ready to use
- Spinach and artichoke dip
- Shredded mozzarella cheese
- Parmesan cheese
- Chopped spinach
- Sliced marinated artichoke hearts

Preparation

1. Preheat the oven to 425°F (220°C). Grease a deep-dish pizza pan with olive oil.
2. Roll out the Chicago pizza dough and press it into the prepared pan, covering the bottom and sides evenly. Let it rest for 10 to 15 minutes.
3. Spread a layer of spinach and artichoke dip evenly on the dough.
4. Sprinkle a generous amount of shredded mozzarella cheese and Parmesan cheese over the dip.
5. Spread the chopped spinach and sliced artichoke hearts over the cheese.
6. Cook the pizza in the oven that has been preheated for approximately 25 to 30 minutes until the crust is golden brown.
7. Remove the pizza from the oven and let it cool for a few minutes before slicing and serving.

Nutritional Values
(per pizza, approximate)

- 1900 cal
- Fat: 100g
- Carbohydrates: 160g
- Protein: 100g

DEEP-DISH PESTO SHRIMP PIZZA

Dough Recipe
Chicago-Style

Ingredients

- Pizza dough (Chicago-style), ready to use
- Basil pesto
- Shredded mozzarella cheese
- Cooked shrimp
- Cherry tomatoes, halved
- Chopped fresh basil

Preparation

1. Preheat the oven to 425°F (220°C). Grease a deep-dish pizza pan with olive oil.
2. Roll out the Chicago pizza dough and press it into the prepared pan, covering the bottom and sides evenly. Let it rest for 10 to 15 minutes.
3. Spread a layer of basil pesto evenly on the dough.
4. Sprinkle a generous amount of shredded mozzarella cheese over the pesto.
5. Spread the cooked shrimp and cherry tomato halves over the cheese.
6. Cook the pizza in the oven that has been preheated for approximately 25 to 30 minutes until the crust is golden brown.
7. Remove the pizza from the oven and sprinkle with chopped fresh basil
8. Let it cool for a few minutes before slicing and serving.

Nutritional Values
(per pizza, approximate)

- 1800 cal
- Fat: 80g
- Carbohydrates: 160g
- Protein: 100g

CHEESY

Cheesy pizzas are a true delight for cheese lovers, offering an explosion of flavors. The perfect dough for these pizzas is the Classic Neapolitan, but if you prefer thin and crispy pizzas, these can also be enjoyed in the New York-style.

These pizzas are typically loaded with a combination of 4 or 5 different cheeses, allowing for endless creativity. They are generously topped with cheeses that are rich in flavor and melt beautifully, such as mozzarella, cheddar, gorgonzola, provolone, fontina, feta, Parmesan, Emmental, and many others.

You can enjoy these pizzas with classic tomato sauce, a creamy white sauce, or even in the traditional Italian style without tomato sauce, allowing the full flavors of the cheeses to shine through.

For the ultimate experience, these pizzas should be served piping hot, and you can even enhance the taste by drizzling a bit of spicy olive oil over them.

SUPREME CHEESY

Dough Recipe
Classic New York-Style

Ingredients
- Pizza dough (New York-Style), ready to use
- Olive oil
- Alfredo sauce
- Shredded mozzarella cheese
- Crumbled Gorgonzola cheese
- Grated Parmesan cheese
- Fresh basil leaves

Preparation
1. Preheat the oven to 475°F (245°C).
2. Roll out the pizza dough into your desired thickness.
3. Place the dough onto a pizza stone or baking sheet.
4. Drizzle olive oil over the dough and spread a thin layer of Alfredo sauce.
5. Sprinkle a layer of shredded mozzarella cheese over the sauce.
6. Distribute crumbled Gorgonzola cheese and grated Parmesan cheese over the mozzarella.
7. Garnish with fresh basil leaves.
8. Bake in the preheated oven for about 12 to 15 minutes or until the crust is golden brown and the cheese is melted and bubbly.
9. Remove from the oven and let it cool for a few minutes before slicing and serving.

Nutritional Values
(per pizza, approximate)
- 1600 cal
- Fat: 90g
- Carbohydrates: 100 g
- Protein: 85g

FOUR CHEESE AND MUSHROOM

Dough Recipe
Classic New York-Style

Ingredients
- Pizza dough (New York-Style), ready to use
- Olive oil
- Tomato sauce
- Shredded mozzarella cheese
- Grated Parmesan cheese
- Crumbled blue cheese
- Sliced provolone cheese
- Sliced mushrooms
- Fresh basil leaves

Preparation
1. Preheat the oven to 475°F (245°C).
2. Roll out the pizza dough into your desired thickness.
3. Place the dough onto a pizza stone or baking sheet.
4. Drizzle olive oil over the dough and spread a thin layer of tomato sauce.
5. Sprinkle a layer of shredded mozzarella cheese, grated Parmesan cheese, crumbled blue cheese, and place slices of provolone cheese.
6. Top with sliced mushrooms and fresh basil leaves.
7. Bake in the preheated oven for about 12 to 15 minutes or until the crust is golden brown and the cheese is melted and bubbly.
8. Remove from the oven and let it cool for a few minutes before slicing and serving.

Nutritional Values
(per pizza, approximate)
- 1900 cal
- Fat: 105g
- Carbohydrates: 125g
- Protein: 85g

FOUR CHEESE PESTO

Dough Recipe
Classic New York-Style

Ingredients

- Pizza dough (New York-Style), ready to use
- Olive oil
- Tomato sauce
- Shredded mozzarella cheese
- Sliced provolone cheese
- Crumbled goat cheese
- Grated Parmesan cheese
- Pesto sauce
- Fresh basil leaves

Preparation
1. Preheat the oven to 475°F (245°C).
2. Roll out the pizza dough into your desired thickness.
3. Place the dough onto a pizza stone or baking sheet.
4. Drizzle olive oil over the dough and spread a thin layer of tomato sauce.
5. Sprinkle a layer of shredded mozzarella cheese and place slices of provolone cheese.
6. Crumble goat cheese over the top.
7. Sprinkle grated Parmesan cheese.
8. Drizzle pesto sauce evenly over the cheese.
9. Scatter fresh basil leaves over the toppings.
10. Bake in the preheated oven for about 12 to 15 minutes or until the crust is golden brown and the cheese is melted and bubbly.
11. Remove from the oven and let it cool for a few minutes before slicing and serving.

Nutritional Values
(per pizza, approximate)
- 2100 cal
- Fat: 120g
- Carbohydrates: 130g
- Protein: 85g

FOUR CHEESE PEPPERONI AND SPINACH

Dough Recipe
Classic New York-Style

Ingredients
- Pizza dough (New York-Style), ready to use
- Olive oil
- Tomato sauce
- Shredded mozzarella cheese
- Sliced provolone cheese
- Crumbled feta cheese
- Grated Parmesan cheese
- Sliced pepperoni
- Fresh spinach leaves
- Garlic powder
- Salt, to taste
- Pepper, to taste

Nutritional Values
(per pizza, approximate)
- 2000 cal
- Fat: 115g
- Carbohydrates: 130g
- Protein: 90g

Preparation
1. Preheat the oven to 475°F (245°C).
2. Roll out the pizza dough into your desired thickness.
3. Place the dough onto a pizza stone or baking sheet.
4. Drizzle olive oil over the dough and spread a thin layer of tomato sauce.
5. Sprinkle a layer of shredded mozzarella cheese and place slices of provolone cheese.
6. Sprinkle crumbled feta cheese and grated Parmesan cheese on top.
7. Add a layer of sliced pepperoni and fresh spinach leaves evenly over the cheese.
8. Season with garlic powder, salt, and pepper to taste.
9. Bake in the preheated oven for about 12 to 15 minutes or until the crust is golden brown and the cheese is melted and bubbly.
10. Remove from the oven and let it cool for a few minutes before slicing and serving.

CALZONE

The calzone is an original Italian specialty, a folded pizza that forms a pocket or envelope. The name "calzone" derives from "big sock" as its shape resembles a sock or shoe. This recipe has ancient roots and is believed to have originated in the 19th century in Southern Italy, particularly in Campania and Puglia.

The traditional preparation of calzone requires a professional wood-fired oven to bake the dough, which is made with flour, salt, water, and yeast. However, you can achieve good results in a home oven with just slightly longer cooking times compared to a classic round pizza.

In Italy, the original calzone recipe calls for a delicious filling of ricotta, provola or mozzarella, fior di latte, salami, Parmesan, and pepper. A popular variation in Neapolitan pizzerias involves covering the calzone with tomato sauce, mozzarella, and basil.

Cooking a homemade calzone requires good experience and knowledge of your own home oven, so it is recommended that you first experiment with traditional pizzas and only challenge yourself with this type of pizza once you have acquired a certain level of skill.

The best dough for these recipes is the Classic Neapolitan Dough.

CLASSIC PEPPERONI CALZONE

Dough Recipe
Classic Neapolitan-Style

Ingredients

- Pizza dough (Neapolitan-style), ready to use
- Tomato sauce
- Shredded mozzarella cheese
- Sliced pepperoni
- Sliced black olives
- Chopped fresh basil
- Dried oregano
- Salt, to taste
- Pepper

Nutritional Values
(per pizza, approximate)

- 1200 cal
- Fat: 60g
- Carbohydrates: 120g
- Protein: 50g

Preparation

1. Preheat the oven to 425°F (220°C).
2. Roll out the calzone dough into a circle or oval shape, about 1/4 inch thick.
3. Spread a layer of tomato sauce on one half of the dough, leaving a border around the edges.
4. Sprinkle a generous amount of shredded mozzarella cheese over the sauce.
5. Add a layer of sliced pepperoni and black olives.
6. Sprinkle chopped fresh basil, dried oregano, salt, and pepper over the toppings.
7. Fold the other half of the dough over the filling and press the edges together to seal.
8. Optional: Use a fork to crimp the edges for a decorative finish.
9. Transfer the calzone onto a baking sheet or pizza stone.
10. Bake in the preheated oven for 15 to 20 minutes or until the crust is golden brown.
11. Remove from the oven and let it cool for a few minutes before serving.

SPINACH AND RICOTTA CALZONE

Dough Recipe
Classic Neapolitan-Style

Ingredients

- Pizza dough (Neapolitan-style), ready to use
- Tomato sauce
- Fresh spinach leaves
- Ricotta cheese
- Shredded mozzarella cheese
- Chopped garlic
- Olive oil
- Salt, to taste
- Pepper, to taste

Nutritional Values
(per pizza, approximate)

- 1100 cal
- Fat: 45g
- Carbohydrates: 130g
- Protein: 45g

Preparation

1. Preheat the oven to 425°F (220°C).
2. Roll out the calzone dough into a circle or oval shape, about 1/4 inch thick.
3. Spread a thin layer of tomato sauce on one half of the dough, leaving a border around the edges.
4. Layer fresh spinach leaves on top of the sauce.
5. Spoon dollops of ricotta cheese over the spinach.
6. Sprinkle shredded mozzarella cheese, chopped garlic, salt, and pepper over the toppings.
7. Drizzle a little olive oil over the filling.
8. Fold the other half of the dough over the filling and press the edges together to seal.
9. Optional: Use a fork to crimp the edges for a decorative finish.
10. Transfer the calzone onto a baking sheet or pizza stone.
11. Bake in the preheated oven for 15 to 20 minutes or until the crust is golden brown.
12. Remove from the oven and let it cool for a few minutes before serving.

BBQ CHICKEN CALZONE

Dough Recipe
Classic Neapolitan-Style

Ingredients

- Pizza dough (Neapolitan-style), ready to use
- BBQ sauce
- Cooked and shredded chicken breast
- Sliced red onions
- Shredded mozzarella cheese
- Chopped fresh cilantro
- Olive oil
- Salt, to taste
- Pepper, to taste

Nutritional Values
(per pizza, approximate)

- 1300 cal
- Fat: 55g
- Carbohydrates: 140g
- Protein: 55g

Preparation

1. Preheat the oven to 425°F (220°C).
2. Roll out the calzone dough into a circle or oval shape, about 1/4 inch thick.
3. Spread a thin layer of BBQ sauce on one half of the dough, leaving a border around the edges.
4. Layer cooked and shredded chicken breast on top of the sauce.
5. Add sliced red onions and shredded mozzarella cheese.
6. Sprinkle chopped fresh cilantro, salt, and pepper over the toppings.
7. Drizzle a little olive oil over the filling.
8. Fold the other half of the dough over the filling and press the edges together to seal.
9. Optional: Use a fork to crimp the edges for a decorative finish.
10. Transfer the calzone onto a baking sheet or pizza stone.
11. Bake in the preheated oven for 15 to 20 minutes or until the crust is golden brown.
12. Remove from the oven and let it cool for a few minutes before serving.

HAM AND CHEESE CALZONE

Dough Recipe
Classic Neapolitan-Style

Ingredients

- Pizza dough (Neapolitan-style), ready to use
- Dijon mustard
- Sliced ham
- Sliced Swiss cheese
- Shredded mozzarella cheese
- Sliced black olives
- Chopped fresh parsley
- Olive oil
- Salt, to taste
- Pepper, to taste

Nutritional Values
(per pizza, approximate)

- 1150 cal
- Fat: 50g
- Carbohydrates: 120g
- Protein: 45g

Preparation

1. Preheat the oven to 425°F (220°C).
2. Roll out the calzone dough into a circle or oval shape, about 1/4 inch thick.
3. Spread a thin layer of Dijon mustard on one half of the dough, leaving a border around the edges.
4. Layer sliced ham and Swiss cheese on top of the mustard.
5. Sprinkle shredded mozzarella cheese, sliced black olives, chopped fresh parsley, salt, and pepper over the toppings.
6. Drizzle a little olive oil over the filling.
7. Fold the other half of the dough over the filling and press the edges together to seal.
8. Optional: Use a fork to crimp the edges for a decorative finish.
9. Transfer the calzone onto a baking sheet or pizza stone.
10. Bake in the preheated oven for 15 to 20 minutes or until the crust is golden brown.
11. Remove from the oven and let it cool for a few minutes before serving.

VEGETARIAN CALZONE

Dough Recipe
Classic Neapolitan-Style

Ingredients

- Pizza dough (Neapolitan-style), ready to use
- Tomato sauce
- Sliced bell peppers (red, green, and yellow)
- Sliced red onions
- Sliced black olives
- Sliced mushrooms
- Chopped fresh basil
- Shredded mozzarella cheese
- Olive oil
- Salt, to taste
- Pepper, to taste

Nutritional Values
(per pizza, approximate)

- 1050 cal
- Fat: 40g
- Carbohydrates: 130g
- Protein: 45g

Preparation

1. Preheat the oven to 425°F (220°C)
2. Roll out the calzone dough into a circle or oval shape, about 1/4 inch thick.
3. Spread a thin layer of tomato sauce on one half of the dough, leaving a border around the edges.
4. Layer sliced bell peppers, red onions, black olives, mushrooms, and chopped fresh basil on top of the sauce.
5. Sprinkle shredded mozzarella cheese, salt, and pepper over the toppings.
6. Drizzle a little olive oil over the filling.
7. Fold the other half of the dough over the filling and press the edges together to seal.
8. Optional: Use a fork to crimp the edges for a decorative finish.
9. Transfer the calzone onto a baking sheet or pizza stone.
10. Bake in the preheated oven for 15 to 20 minutes or until the crust is golden brown.
11. Remove from the oven and let it cool for a few minutes before serving.

CHICKEN AND BROCCOLI CALZONE

Dough Recipe
Classic Neapolitan-Style

Ingredients

- Pizza dough (Neapolitan-style), ready to use
- Alfredo sauce
- Cooked and shredded chicken breast
- Steamed broccoli florets
- Shredded mozzarella cheese
- Chopped garlic
- Olive oil
- Salt, to taste
- Pepper, to taste

Nutritional Values
(per pizza, approximate)

- 1200 cal
- Fat: 50g
- Carbohydrates: 140g
- Protein: 50g

Preparation

1. Preheat the oven to 425°F (220°C).
2. Roll out the calzone dough into a circle or oval shape, about 1/4 inch thick.
3. Spread a thin layer of Alfredo sauce on one half of the dough, leaving a border around the edges.
4. Layer cooked and shredded chicken breast and steamed broccoli florets on top of the sauce.
5. Sprinkle shredded mozzarella cheese, chopped garlic, salt, and pepper over the toppings.
6. Drizzle a little olive oil over the filling.
7. Fold the other half of the dough over the filling and press the edges together to seal.
8. Optional: Use a fork to crimp the edges for a decorative finish.
9. Transfer the calzone onto a baking sheet or pizza stone.
10. Bake in the preheated oven for 15 to 20 minutes or until the crust is golden brown.
11. Remove from the oven and let it cool for a few minutes before serving.

BBQ PORK CALZONE

Dough Recipe
Classic Neapolitan-Style

Ingredients
- Pizza dough (Neapolitan-style), ready to use
- BBQ sauce
- Pulled pork
- Sliced red onions
- Shredded mozzarella cheese
- Chopped fresh cilantro
- Olive oil
- Salt to taste
- Pepper, to taste

Nutritional Values
(per pizza, approximate)
- 1100 cal
- Fat: 45g
- Carbohydrates: 140g
- Protein: 45g

Preparation
1. Preheat the oven to 425°F (220°C).
2. Roll out the calzone dough into a circle or oval shape, about 1/4 inch thick.
3. Spread a thin layer of BBQ sauce on one half of the dough, leaving a border around the edges.
4. Layer pulled pork and sliced red onions on top of the sauce.
5. Sprinkle shredded mozzarella cheese, chopped fresh cilantro, salt, and pepper over the toppings.
6. Drizzle a little olive oil over the filling.
7. Fold the other half of the dough over the filling and press the edges together to seal.
8. Optional: Use a fork to crimp the edges for a decorative finish.
9. Transfer the calzone onto a baking sheet or pizza stone.
10. Bake in the preheated oven for 15 to 20 minutes or until the crust is golden brown.
11. Remove from the oven and let it cool for a few minutes before serving.

MEDITERRANEAN CALZONE

Dough Recipe
Classic Neapolitan-Style

Ingredients
- Pizza dough (Neapolitan-style), ready to use
- Tomato sauce
- Sliced black olives
- Sliced sun-dried tomatoes
- Chopped fresh basil
- Crumbled feta cheese
- Shredded mozzarella cheese
- Olive oil
- Salt, to taste
- Pepper, to taste

Nutritional Values
(per pizza, approximate)
- 1000 cal
- Fat: 40g
- Carbohydrates: 130g
- Protein: 40g

Preparation
1. Preheat the oven to 425°F (220°C).
2. Roll out the calzone dough into a circle or oval shape, about 1/4 inch thick.
3. Spread a thin layer of tomato sauce on one half of the dough, leaving a border around the edges.
4. Layer sliced black olives, sun-dried tomatoes, chopped fresh basil, crumbled feta cheese, salt, and pepper on top of the sauce.
5. Sprinkle shredded mozzarella cheese over the toppings.
6. Drizzle a little olive oil over the filling.
7. Fold the other half of the dough over the filling and press the edges together to seal.
8. Optional: Use a fork to crimp the edges for a decorative finish.
9. Transfer the calzone onto a baking sheet or pizza stone.
10. Bake in the preheated oven for 15 to 20 minutes or until the crust is golden brown.
11. Remove from the oven and let it cool for a few minutes before serving.

CURRY CALZONE

Dough Recipe
Classic Neapolitan-Style

Ingredients
- Pizza dough (Neapolitan-style), ready to use
- 1 cup cooked curry chicken, shredded
- 0.5 cup sliced bell peppers
- 0.25 cup sliced red onion
- 0.25 tsp chili pepper flakes
- 1 cup shredded mozzarella cheese
- Fresh cilantro leaves

Nutritional Values
(per pizza, approximate)
- 1000 cal
- Fat: 40g
- Carbohydrates: 130g
- Protein: 40g

Preparation
1. Preheat the oven to 425°F (220°C).
2. Roll out the calzone dough into a circle or oval shape, about 1/4 inch thick.
3. Spread the cooked curry chicken evenly over half of the dough, leaving a small border.
4. Top the chicken with sliced bell peppers, red onion, chili pepper flakes, and shredded mozzarella cheese.
5. Fold the other half of the dough over the filling and press the edges to seal.
6. Transfer the calzone to a baking sheet and bake in the preheated oven until golden brown and crispy.
7. Remove from the oven and let it cool for a few minutes before serving. Garnish with fresh cilantro leaves.

PHILLY CHEESESTEAK CALZONE

Dough Recipe
Classic Neapolitan-Style

Ingredients
- Pizza dough (Neapolitan-style), ready to use
- Thinly-sliced ribeye steak
- Sliced green bell peppers
- Sliced onions
- Provolone cheese, sliced or shredded
- Olive oil
- Salt, to taste
- Pepper, to taste

Nutritional Values
(per pizza, approximate)
- 1300 cal
- Fat: 60g
- Carbohydrates: 110g
- Protein: 65g

Preparation
1. Preheat the oven to 425°F (220°C).
2. Roll out the calzone dough into a circle or oval shape, about 1/4 inch thick.
3. Layer thinly-sliced ribeye steak, sliced green bell peppers, and sliced onions on one half of the dough, leaving a border around the edges.
4. Sprinkle salt and pepper over the filling.
5. Place provolone cheese slices or shredded provolone cheese on top of the filling.
6. Drizzle a little olive oil over the filling.
7. Fold the other half of the dough over the filling and press the edges together to seal.
8. Optional: Use a fork to crimp the edges for a decorative finish.
9. Transfer the calzone onto a baking sheet or pizza stone.
10. Bake in the preheated oven for 15 to 20 minutes or until the crust is golden brown.
11. Remove from the oven and let it cool for a few minutes before serving.

CHICKEN ALFREDO CALZONE

Dough Recipe
Classic Neapolitan-Style

Ingredients
- Pizza dough (Neapolitan-style), ready to use
- Alfredo sauce
- Cooked and shredded chicken breast
- Chopped fresh spinach
- Minced garlic
- Shredded mozzarella cheese
- Olive oil
- Salt, to taste
- Pepper, to taste

Nutritional Values
(per pizza, approximate)
- 1250 cal
- Fat: 50g
- Carbohydrates: 130g
- Protein: 55g

Preparation
1. Preheat the oven to 425°F (220°C).
2. Roll out the calzone dough into a circle or oval shape, about 1/4 inch thick.
3. Spread a thin layer of Alfredo sauce on one half of the dough, leaving a border around the edges.
4. Layer cooked and shredded chicken breast, chopped fresh spinach, minced garlic, salt, and pepper on top of the sauce.
5. Sprinkle shredded mozzarella cheese over the toppings.
6. Drizzle a little olive oil over the filling.
7. Fold the other half of the dough over the filling and press the edges together to seal.
8. Optional: Use a fork to crimp the edges for a decorative finish.
9. Transfer the calzone onto a baking sheet or pizza stone.
10. Bake in the preheated oven for 15 to 20 minutes or until the crust is golden brown.
11. Remove from the oven and let it cool for a few minutes before serving.

MEXICAN CALZONE

Dough Recipe
Classic Neapolitan-Style

Ingredients
- Pizza dough (Neapolitan-style), ready to use
- 0.5 cup cooked spicy ground beef
- 0.25 cup black beans
- 0.25 cup shredded cheddar cheese
- 0.25 cup sliced jalapeno peppers
- 0.25 cup diced tomatoes
- Fresh cilantro leaves

Preparation
1. Preheat the oven to 425°F (220°C).
2. Roll out the calzone dough into a circle or oval shape, about 1/4 inch thick.
3. Spread the cooked spicy ground beef evenly over half of the dough, leaving a small border.
4. Top the beef with black beans, shredded cheddar cheese, sliced jalapeno peppers, and diced tomatoes.
5. Fold the other half of the dough over the filling and press the edges to seal.
6. Transfer the calzone to a baking sheet and bake in the preheated oven until the crust is golden brown and crispy.
7. Remove from the oven and let it cool for a few minutes before serving. Garnish with fresh cilantro leaves.

Nutritional Values
(per pizza, approximate)
- 1100 cal
- Fat: 50g
- Carbohydrates: 130g
- Protein: 55g

HAWAIIAN CALZONE

Dough Recipe
Classic Neapolitan-Style

Ingredients

- Pizza dough (Neapolitan-style), ready to use
- Tomato sauce
- Sliced ham
- Pineapple tidbits
- Shredded mozzarella cheese
- Olive oil
- Salt, to taste
- Pepper, to taste

Nutritional Values
(per pizza, approximate)

- 1100 cal
- Fat: 40g
- Carbohydrates: 130g
- Protein: 45g

Preparation

1. Preheat the oven to 425°F (220°C).
2. Roll out the calzone dough into a circle or oval shape, about 1/4 inch thick.
3. Spread a thin layer of tomato sauce on one half of the dough, leaving a border around the edges.
4. Layer sliced ham and pineapple tidbits on top of the sauce.
5. Sprinkle shredded mozzarella cheese, salt, and pepper over the toppings.
6. Drizzle a little olive oil over the filling.
7. Fold the other half of the dough over the filling and press the edges together to seal.
8. Optional: Use a fork to crimp the edges for a decorative finish.
9. Transfer the calzone onto a baking sheet or pizza stone.
10. Bake in the preheated oven for 15 to 20 minutes or until the crust is golden brown.
11. Remove from the oven and let it cool for a few minutes before serving.

VEGAN CALZONE

Dough Recipe
Classic Neapolitan-Style

Ingredients

- Pizza dough (Neapolitan-style), ready to use
- 1 cup smoked tofu, sliced
- 0.5 cup mixed mushrooms, sliced
- 1 cup fresh spinach leaves
- 0.25 cup sliced onion
- 0.25 cup sun-dried tomatoes, chopped
- 0.5 cup vegan cheese, shredded

Preparation

1. Preheat the oven to 425°F (220°C).
2. Roll out the calzone dough into a circle or oval shape, about 1/4 inch thick.
3. Arrange the smoked tofu, mixed mushrooms, fresh spinach, sliced onion, and sun-dried tomatoes on half of the dough.
4. Sprinkle the vegan cheese over the filling.
5. Fold the other half of the dough over the filling and press the edges to seal.
6. Place the calzone on a baking sheet and bake in the preheated oven until the crust is golden brown and crispy.
7. Allow the calzone to cool for a few minutes before serving.

Nutritional Values
(per pizza, approximate)

- 1250 cal
- Fat: 50g
- Carbohydrates: 130g
- Protein: 55g

SEAFOOD CALZONE

Dough Recipe
Classic Neapolitan-Style

Ingredients
- Pizza dough (Neapolitan-style), ready to use
- 0.5 cup cooked shrimp, peeled and deveined
- 0.5 cup cooked calamari rings
- 0.5 cup cooked mussels, shelled
- 0.5 cup tomato sauce
- 1 cup shredded mozzarella cheese
- 2 cloves garlic, minced
- Fresh parsley leaves

Nutritional Values
(per pizza, approximate)
- 1100 cal
- Fat: 40g
- Carbohydrates: 130g
- Protein: 45g

Preparation
1. Preheat the oven to 425°F (220°C).
2. Roll out the calzone dough into a circle or oval shape, about 1/4 inch thick.
3. Spread the tomato sauce evenly over half of the dough, leaving a small border.
4. Top the sauce with cooked shrimp, calamari rings, mussels, minced garlic, and shredded mozzarella cheese.
5. Fold the other half of the dough over the filling and press the edges to seal.
6. Place the calzone on a baking sheet and bake in the preheated oven until the crust is golden brown and crispy.
7. Allow the calzone to cool for a few minutes before serving. Garnish with fresh parsley leaves.

CAPRESE CALZONE

Dough Recipe
Classic Neapolitan-Style

Ingredients
- Pizza dough (Neapolitan-style), ready to use
- Tomato sauce
- Fresh mozzarella cheese, sliced
- Cherry tomatoes, halved
- Fresh basil leaves
- Olive oil
- Salt, to taste
- Pepper, to taste

Nutritional Values
(per pizza, approximate)
- 1050 cal
- Fat: 35g
- Carbohydrates: 130g
- Protein: 45g

Preparation
1. Preheat the oven to 425°F (220°C).
2. Roll out the calzone dough into a circle or oval shape, about 1/4 inch thick.
3. Spread a thin layer of tomato sauce on one half of the dough, leaving a border around the edges.
4. Layer fresh mozzarella cheese slices, cherry tomato halves, and fresh basil leaves on top of the sauce.
5. Drizzle a little olive oil over the filling and sprinkle with salt and pepper.
6. Fold the other half of the dough over the filling and press the edges together to seal.
7. Optional: Use a fork to crimp the edges for a decorative finish.
8. Transfer the calzone onto a baking sheet or pizza stone.
9. Bake in the preheated oven for 15 to 20 minutes or until the crust is golden brown.
10. Remove from the oven and let it cool for a few minutes before serving.

MEATBALL AND RICOTTA CALZONE

Dough Recipe
Classic Neapolitan-Style

Ingredients
- Pizza dough (Neapolitan-style), ready to use
- Tomato sauce
- Cooked meatballs, sliced
- Ricotta cheese
- Shredded mozzarella cheese
- Grated Parmesan cheese
- Chopped fresh basil
- Olive oil
- Salt, to taste
- Pepper, to taste

Nutritional Values
(per pizza, approximate)
- 1200 cal
- Fat: 45g
- Carbohydrates: 130g
- Protein: 55g

Preparation
1. Preheat the oven to 425°F (220°C).
2. Roll out the calzone dough into a circle or oval shape, about 1/4 inch thick.
3. Spread a thin layer of tomato sauce on one half of the dough, leaving a border around the edges.
4. Layer sliced cooked meatballs, ricotta cheese, shredded mozzarella cheese, grated Parmesan cheese, and chopped fresh basil on top of the sauce.
5. Drizzle a little olive oil over the filling and sprinkle with salt and pepper.
6. Fold the other half of the dough over the filling and press the edges together to seal.
7. Optional: Use a fork to crimp the edges for a decorative finish.
8. Transfer the calzone onto a baking sheet or pizza stone.
9. Bake in the preheated oven for 15 to 20 minutes or until the crust is golden brown.
10. Remove from the oven and let it cool for a few minutes before serving.

PRIMAVERA CALZONE

Dough Recipe
Classic Neapolitan-Style

Ingredients
- Pizza dough (Neapolitan-style), ready to use
- 1 cup asparagus, trimmed and sliced
- 0.5 cup peas
- 0.5 cup green beans, trimmed and chopped
- 0.5 cup crumbled goat cheese
- 2 cloves garlic, minced
- Fresh mint leaves
- Salt, to taste
- Pepper, to taste

Nutritional Values
(per pizza, approximate)
- 1000 cal
- Fat: 40g
- Carbohydrates: 130g
- Protein: 50g

Preparation
1. Preheat the oven to 425°F (220°C).
2. Roll out the calzone dough into a circle or oval shape, about 1/4 inch thick.
3. In a bowl, combine the sliced asparagus, peas, green beans, crumbled goat cheese, minced garlic, salt, and pepper.
4. Spread the vegetable and cheese mixture over half of the dough, leaving a small border.
5. Fold the other half of the dough over the filling and press the edges to seal.
6. Transfer the calzone to a baking sheet and bake in the preheated oven until the crust is golden brown.
7. Remove from the oven and let it cool slightly before serving. Garnish with fresh mint leaves.

CHEESY VEGGIE CALZONE

Dough Recipe
Classic Neapolitan-Style

Ingredients
- Pizza dough (Neapolitan-style), ready to use
- Tomato sauce
- Shredded mozzarella cheese
- Sliced bell peppers (assorted colors)
- Sliced red onions
- Sliced black olives
- Sliced mushrooms
- Chopped fresh basil
- Olive oil
- Salt, to taste
- Pepper, to taste

Nutritional Values
(per pizza, approximate)
- 1100 cal
- Fat: 35g
- Carbohydrates: 130g
- Protein: 45g

Preparation
1. Preheat the oven to 425°F (220°C).
2. Roll out the calzone dough into a circle or oval shape, about 1/4 inch thick.
3. Spread a thin layer of tomato sauce on one half of the dough, leaving a border around the edges.
4. Sprinkle a generous amount of shredded mozzarella cheese over the sauce.
5. Layer sliced bell peppers, red onions, black olives, sliced mushrooms, and chopped fresh basil on top of the cheese.
6. Drizzle a little olive oil over the filling and sprinkle with salt and pepper.
7. Fold the other half of the dough over the filling and press the edges together to seal.
8. Optional: Use a fork to crimp the edges for a decorative finish.
9. Transfer the calzone onto a baking sheet or pizza stone.
10. Bake in the preheated oven for 15 to 20 minutes or until the crust is golden brown.
11. Remove from the oven and let it cool for a few minutes before serving.

MIDDLE EASTERN CALZONE

Dough Recipe
Classic Neapolitan-Style

Ingredients
- Pizza dough (Neapolitan-style), ready to use
- 1 cup grilled chicken, sliced
- 0.25 cup hummus
- 0.25 cup sun-dried tomatoes, chopped
- 0.25 cup black olives, sliced
- 0.25 cup crumbled feta cheese
- Fresh parsley leaves

Preparation
1. Preheat the oven to 425°F (220°C).
2. Roll out the pizza dough on a lightly floured surface into a round shape.
3. Spread the hummus evenly over half of the dough, leaving a small border.
4. Top the hummus with grilled chicken, sun-dried tomatoes, black olives, and crumbled feta cheese.
5. Fold the other half of the dough over the filling and press the edges to seal.
6. Transfer the calzone to a baking sheet and bake in the preheated oven until the crust is golden brown and crispy.
7. Remove from the oven and let it cool for a few minutes before serving. Garnish with fresh parsley leaves.

Nutritional Values
(per pizza, approximate)
- 1100 cal
- Fat: 40g
- Carbohydrates: 130g
- Protein: 50g

PIZZA FRITTA

Fried pizza, also known as "montanara pizza" or "Neapolitan fried pizza," is a culinary specialty that originates from the Neapolitan tradition in Italy. It is a variation of pizza that is fried instead of being baked in the oven.

Fried pizza has ancient origins and represents one of the earliest known forms of pizza. Traditionally, the dough for fried pizza is similar to that of classic Neapolitan pizza but is fried in hot oil instead of being baked. The dough is shaped into a circular or rectangular form, then immersed in hot oil until it becomes golden and crispy.

After frying, the pizza is topped with a variety of raw ingredients. The fillings can include tomatoes, mozzarella, ricotta, cold cuts, vegetables, and various cheeses.

Another way to prepare fried pizza is by rolling out the dough into a round shape, filling one half, and folding it over like a calzone. In this variation, the calzone is fried in deep, hot oil until it turns golden in color.

Fried pizza is loved for its crispy exterior and soft interior, as well as the intense flavors of its ingredients. It is often served hot, right after frying, and is considered a delicacy to be enjoyed on-site or taken away.

Today, fried pizza is widely appreciated not only in Italy but also in many other parts of the world. It has gained popularity as street food and is available in various regional and local variations.

FRIED MARGHERITA PIZZA

Dough Recipe
Classic Neapolitan-Style

Ingredients
- 0.5 batch of Classic Neapolitan Dough
- Tomato sauce
- Fresh mozzarella cheese, sliced
- Fresh basil leaves
- Olive oil
- Salt, to taste
- Vegetable oil for frying

Nutritional Values
(per pizza, approximate)
- 920 cal
- Fat: 48g
- Carbohydrates: 88g
- Protein: 33g

Preparation
1. Prepare the Classic Neapolitan Dough according to the base recipe.
2. Take a dough ball and flatten it with your hands, forming a disk about 4 to 6 inches in diameter.
3. Spread a spoonful of tomato sauce on the dough, leaving a border around the edges.
4. Place a few slices of fresh mozzarella cheese on top of the sauce.
5. Tear some fresh basil leaves and distribute them over the cheese.
6. Drizzle a little olive oil over the toppings and sprinkle with salt.
7. Fold the other half of the dough over the toppings and seal the edges tightly.
8. Heat vegetable oil in a deep fryer or a large pan to about 375°F (190°C).
9. Carefully place the folded pizza into the hot oil and fry until golden brown on both sides.
10. Remove the fried pizza from the oil and let it drain on paper towels.
11. Repeat the process with the remaining dough and toppings.
12. Serve the fried Margherita pizza hot and enjoy!

FRIED NAPOLI PIZZA

Dough Recipe
Classic Neapolitan-Style

Ingredients
- 0.5 batch of Classic Neapolitan Dough
- Tomato sauce
- Mozzarella cheese
- Anchovies
- Dried oregano
- Vegetable oil for frying

Nutritional Values
(per pizza, approximate)
- 920 cal
- Fat: 45g
- Carbohydrates: 100g
- Protein: 25g

Preparation
1. Prepare the Classic Neapolitan Dough according to the base recipe.
2. Take a dough ball and flatten it with your hands, forming a disk about 4 to 6 inches in diameter.
3. Spread a spoonful of tomato sauce on the dough, leaving a border around the edges.
4. Place slices of mozzarella cheese on top of the sauce.
5. Arrange anchovies on the cheese.
6. Sprinkle dried oregano over the toppings.
7. Fold the other half of the dough over the toppings and seal the edges tightly.
8. Heat vegetable oil in a deep fryer or a large pan to about 375°F (190°C).
9. Carefully place the folded pizza into the hot oil and fry until golden brown on both sides.
10. Remove the fried pizza from the oil and let it drain on paper towels.
11. Serve the fried Napoli pizza hot and enjoy!

FRIED FOUR CHEESE PIZZA

Dough Recipe
Classic Neapolitan-Style

Ingredients
- 0.5 batch of Classic Neapolitan Dough
- Tomato sauce
- Mozzarella cheese
- Gorgonzola cheese
- Pecorino cheese
- Parmesan cheese
- Vegetable oil for frying

Nutritional Values
(per pizza, approximate)
- 990 cal
- Fat: 50g
- Carbohydrates: 95g
- Protein: 35g

Preparation
1. Prepare the Classic Neapolitan Dough according to the base recipe.
2. Take a dough ball and flatten it with your hands, forming a disk about 4 to 6 inches in diameter.
3. Take a dough ball and flatten it with your hands, forming a disk about 4 to 6 inches in diameter.
4. Spread a spoonful of tomato sauce on the dough, leaving a border around the edges.
5. Sprinkle a combination of mozzarella, gorgonzola, pecorino, and parmesan cheeses on top of the sauce.
6. Fold the other half of the dough over the toppings and seal the edges tightly.
7. Heat vegetable oil in a deep fryer or a large pan to about 375°F (190°C).
8. Carefully place the folded pizza into the hot oil and fry until golden brown on both sides.
9. Remove the fried pizza from the oil and let it drain on paper towels.
10. Serve the fried four cheese pizza hot and enjoy!

FRIED CAPRICCIOSA PIZZA

Dough Recipe
Classic Neapolitan-Style

Ingredients
- 0.5 batch of Classic Neapolitan Dough
- Tomato sauce
- Mozzarella cheese
- Mushrooms
- Cooked ham
- Artichokes
- Olives
- Vegetable oil for frying

Nutritional Values
(per pizza, approximate)
- 980 cal
- Fat: 40g
- Carbohydrates: 115g
- Protein: 30g

Preparation
1. Prepare the Classic Neapolitan Dough according to the base recipe.
2. Take a dough ball and flatten it with your hands, forming a disk about 4 to 6 inches in diameter.
3. Spread a spoonful of tomato sauce on the dough, leaving a border around the edges.
4. Place slices of mozzarella cheese on top of the sauce.
5. Arrange mushrooms, cooked ham, artichokes, and olives on the cheese.
6. Fold the other half of the dough over the toppings and seal the edges tightly.
7. Heat vegetable oil in a deep fryer or a large pan to about 375°F (190°C).
8. Carefully place the folded pizza into the hot oil and fry until golden brown on both sides.
9. Remove the fried pizza from the oil and let it drain on paper towels.
10. Serve the fried Capricciosa pizza hot and enjoy!

FRIED VEGGIE DELIGHT PIZZA

Dough Recipe
Classic Neapolitan-Style

Ingredients
- 0.5 batch of Classic Neapolitan Dough
- Tomato sauce
- Shredded mozzarella cheese
- Sliced bell peppers (red, green, and yellow)
- Sliced red onions
- Sliced black olives
- Sliced mushrooms
- Vegetable oil for frying

Nutritional Values
(per pizza, approximate)
- 840 cal
- Fat: 45g
- Carbohydrates: 88g
- Protein: 30g

Preparation
1. Prepare the Classic Neapolitan Dough according to the base recipe.
2. Take a dough ball and flatten it with your hands, forming a disk about 4 to 6 inches in diameter.
3. Spread a spoonful of tomato sauce on the dough, leaving a border around the edges.
4. Sprinkle a generous amount of shredded mozzarella cheese over the sauce.
5. Arrange the sliced bell peppers, red onions, black olives, and mushrooms on top of the cheese.
6. Fold the other half of the dough over the toppings and seal the edges tightly.
7. Heat vegetable oil in a deep fryer or a large pan to about 375°F (190°C).
8. Carefully place the folded pizza into the hot oil and fry until golden brown on both sides.
9. Remove the fried pizza from the oil and let it drain on paper towels.
10. Repeat the process with the remaining dough and toppings.
11. Serve the fried veggie delight pizza hot and enjoy!

FRIED PROSCIUTTO AND ARUGULA PIZZA

Dough Recipe
Classic Neapolitan-Style

Ingredients
- 0.5 batch of Classic Neapolitan Dough
- Tomato sauce
- Mozzarella cheese
- Ham
- Fresh arugula
- Vegetable oil for frying

Nutritional Values
(per pizza, approximate)
- 940 cal
- Fat: 35g
- Carbohydrates: 110g
- Protein: 35g

Preparation
1. Prepare the Classic Neapolitan Dough according to the base recipe.
2. Take a dough ball and flatten it with your hands, forming a disk about 4 to 6 inches in diameter.
3. Spread a spoonful of tomato sauce on the dough, leaving a border around the edges.
4. Place slices of mozzarella cheese on top of the sauce.
5. Arrange ham slices on the cheese.
6. Top with a handful of fresh arugula.
7. Fold the other half of the dough over the toppings and seal the edges tightly.
8. Heat vegetable oil in a deep fryer or a large pan to about 375°F (190°C).
9. Carefully place the folded pizza into the hot oil and fry until golden brown on both sides.
10. Remove the fried pizza from the oil and let it drain on paper towels.
11. Serve the fried ham and arugula pizza hot and enjoy!

FRIED TUNA AND ONION PIZZA

Dough Recipe
Classic Neapolitan-Style

Ingredients
- 0.5 batch of Classic Neapolitan Dough
- Tomato sauce
- Mozzarella cheese
- Canned tuna in oil
- Sliced onion
- Vegetable oil for frying

Nutritional Values
(per pizza, approximate)
- 890 cal
- Fat: 40g
- Carbohydrates: 95g
- Protein: 30g

Preparation
1. Prepare the Classic Neapolitan Dough according to the base recipe.
2. Take a dough ball and flatten it with your hands, forming a disk about 4 to 6 inches in diameter.
3. Spread a spoonful of tomato sauce on the dough, leaving a border around the edges.
4. Place slices of mozzarella cheese on top of the sauce.
5. Distribute the canned tuna evenly over the cheese.
6. Arrange slices of onion on top of the tuna.
7. Fold the other half of the dough over the toppings and seal the edges tightly.
8. Heat vegetable oil in a deep fryer or a large pan to about 375°F (190°C).
9. Carefully place the folded pizza into the hot oil and fry until golden brown on both sides.
10. Remove the fried pizza from the oil and let it drain on paper towels.
11. Serve the fried tuna and onion pizza hot and enjoy!

FRIED PEPPERONI AND MUSHROOM PIZZA

Dough Recipe
Classic Neapolitan-Style

Ingredients
- 0.5 batch of Classic Neapolitan Dough
- Tomato sauce
- Shredded mozzarella cheese
- Sliced pepperoni
- Sliced mushrooms
- Vegetable oil for frying

Nutritional Values
(per pizza, approximate)
- 920 cal
- Fat: 48g
- Carbohydrates: 88g
- Protein: 33g

Preparation
1. Prepare the Classic Neapolitan Dough according to the base recipe.
2. Take a dough ball and flatten it with your hands, forming a disk about 4 to 6 inches in diameter.
3. Spread a spoonful of tomato sauce on the dough, leaving a border around the edges.
4. Sprinkle a generous amount of shredded mozzarella cheese over the sauce.
5. Place slices of pepperoni and mushrooms on top of the cheese.
6. Fold the other half of the dough over the toppings and seal the edges tightly.
7. Heat vegetable oil in a deep fryer or a large pan to about 375°F (190°C).
8. Carefully place the folded pizza into the hot oil and fry until golden brown on both sides.
9. Repeat the process with the remaining dough and toppings.
10. Serve the fried pepperoni and mushroom pizza hot and enjoy!

FRIED BBQ CHICKEN PIZZA

Dough Recipe
Classic Neapolitan-Style

Ingredients
- 0.5 batch of Classic Neapolitan Dough
- BBQ sauce
- Shredded mozzarella cheese
- Cooked and shredded chicken
- Sliced red onions
- Chopped cilantro
- Vegetable oil for frying

Nutritional Values
(per pizza, approximate)
- 940 cal
- Fat: 52g
- Carbohydrates: 80g
- Protein: 39g

Preparation
1. Prepare the Classic Neapolitan Dough according to the base recipe.
2. Take a dough ball and flatten it with your hands, forming a disk about 4 to 6 inches in diameter.
3. Spread a spoonful of BBQ sauce on the dough, leaving a border around the edges.
4. Sprinkle a generous amount of shredded mozzarella cheese over the sauce.
5. Add the cooked and shredded chicken, sliced red onions, and chopped cilantro on top of the cheese.
6. Fold the other half of the dough over the toppings and seal the edges tightly.
7. Heat vegetable oil in a deep fryer or a large pan to about 375°F (190°C).
8. Carefully place the folded pizza into the hot oil and fry until golden brown on both sides.
9. Remove the fried pizza from the oil and let it drain on paper towels.
10. Repeat the process with the remaining dough and toppings.
11. Serve the fried BBQ chicken pizza hot and enjoy!

FRIED CAPRESE PIZZA

Dough Recipe
Classic Neapolitan-Style

Ingredients
- 0.5 batch of Classic Neapolitan Dough
- Tomato sauce
- Sliced fresh mozzarella cheese
- Sliced tomatoes
- Fresh basil leaves
- Balsamic glaze
- Vegetable oil for frying

Nutritional Values
(per pizza, approximate)
- 780 cal
- Fat: 38g
- Carbohydrates: 80g
- Protein: 29g

Preparation
1. Prepare the Classic Neapolitan Dough according to the base recipe.
2. Take a dough ball and flatten it with your hands, forming a disk about 4 to 6 inches in diameter.
3. Spread a spoonful of tomato sauce on the dough, leaving a border around the edges.
4. Arrange slices of fresh mozzarella cheese and tomatoes on top of the sauce.
5. Place fresh basil leaves on the cheese and drizzle balsamic glaze over the toppings.
6. Fold the other half of the dough over the toppings and seal the edges tightly.
7. Heat vegetable oil in a deep fryer or a large pan to about 375°F (190°C).
8. Carefully place the folded pizza into the hot oil and fry until golden brown on both sides.
9. Remove the fried pizza from the oil and let it drain on paper towels.
10. Repeat the process with the remaining dough and toppings.
11. Serve the fried Caprese pizza hot and enjoy!

FOCACCIA

Focaccia is a type of Italian flatbread known for its soft and slightly crispy texture. It originated in Italy, particularly in the Liguria region, although it is popular throughout the country and has many regional variations.

Focaccia is made with a simple mixture of flour, water, yeast, olive oil, and salt. The dough is kneaded and then stretched out on a baking sheet, where it is allowed to rise before being baked.

In the classic recipe, during baking, the surface of the focaccia is brushed with olive oil and often topped with coarse salt and other additions such as rosemary, olives, onions, or cherry tomatoes. However, focaccia can also be topped with other ingredients or sliced in half and used as a bread substitute to create delicious sandwiches.

Its preparation is highly versatile and appreciated for its delicate flavor and tall, fluffy texture. Each Italian region has its own characteristic version of focaccia, each with slight variations in ingredients and preparation methods.

Focaccia Dough Recipe

Ingredient:

- 4 cups durum wheat flour

- 1.25 cups water

- 1 tbsp fresh yeast

- 2 tsp salt

- 0.25 cup of extra-virgin olive oil

Start by dissolving the fresh yeast in warm water and let it rest for a few minutes until it becomes frothy. In a large bowl, pour the durum wheat flour and add the activated yeast.

Add the salt and extra-virgin olive oil. Mix the ingredients with a spatula or your hands until they form a homogeneous dough.

Transfer the dough to a lightly floured surface and knead it vigorously for about 10 minutes until it becomes smooth and elastic.

Shape the dough into a ball and place it in a lightly oiled bowl. Cover with a damp cloth and let it rise in a warm place for about 1 to 2 hours or until it doubles in size.

Once the dough has risen, take it out and flatten it with your hands on an oiled baking sheet.

Cover the baking sheet with a damp cloth and let it rise for another 30 to 45 minutes.

Preheat the oven to 425°F (220°C) while the dough rises. Bake the focaccia for about 20 to 25 minutes or until it turns golden and crispy.

Once it's baked, remove the focaccia from the oven and let it cool slightly before cutting it into slices and serving.

CLASSIC FOCACCIA

Dough Recipe
Classic Focaccia Dough

Ingredients
- Classic focaccia dough, ready to use
- 0.25 cup olive oil
- 2 tsp coarse salt
- 2 tbsp fresh rosemary leaves

Nutritional Values
(per pizza, approximate)
- 180 cal
- Fat: 6g
- Carbohydrates: 27g
- Protein: 4g

Preparation
1. Preheat the oven to 425°F (220°C).
2. Take the prepared Classic Focaccia Dough and transfer it to a greased baking sheet or a rectangular baking pan.
3. Gently stretch and press the dough to fit the pan, creating an even layer.
4. Drizzle the olive oil evenly over the surface of the dough.
5. Use your fingertips to create dimples in the dough, allowing the oil to fill the indentations.
6. Sprinkle the coarse salt and fresh rosemary leaves over the top, distributing them evenly.
7. Bake in the preheated oven for about 20 to 25 minutes or until the focaccia is golden brown on top.
8. Remove from the oven and let it cool for a few minutes before slicing and serving.

POTATO AND ROSEMARY FOCACCIA

Dough Recipe
Classic Focaccia Dough

Ingredients
- Classic focaccia dough, ready to use
- 2 or 3 medium-sized potatoes, thinly sliced
- 2 tbsp fresh rosemary leaves
- 0.25 cup olive oil
- 1 tsp coarse salt

Preparation
1. Preheat the oven to 425°F (220°C).
2. Take the prepared Classic Focaccia Dough and transfer it to a greased baking sheet or a rectangular baking pan.
3. Gently stretch and press the dough to fit the pan, creating an even layer.
4. Arrange the thinly sliced potatoes evenly over the dough.
5. Sprinkle fresh rosemary leaves, coarse salt, and drizzle olive oil over the top.
6. Bake in the preheated oven for about 20 to 25 minutes or until the focaccia is golden brown and the potatoes are tender.
7. Remove from the oven and let it cool for a few minutes before slicing and serving.

Nutritional Values
(per pizza, approximate)
- 220 cal
- Fat: 8g
- Carbohydrates: 33g
- Protein: 5g

GARLIC AND PARMESAN FOCACCIA

Dough Recipe
Classic Focaccia Dough

Ingredients
- Classic focaccia dough, ready to use
- 3 or 4 cloves garlic, minced
- 0.5 cup grated Parmesan cheese
- 0.25 cup olive oil
- 1 tsp coarse salt

Preparation
1. Preheat the oven to 425°F (220°C).
2. Take the prepared Classic Focaccia Dough and transfer it to a greased baking sheet or a rectangular baking pan.
3. Gently stretch and press the dough to fit the pan, creating an even layer.
4. Sprinkle minced garlic and grated Parmesan cheese evenly over the dough.
5. Drizzle olive oil over the top and sprinkle coarse salt.
6. Bake in the preheated oven for about 20 to 25 minutes or until the focaccia is golden brown and the cheese is melted and bubbly.
7. Remove from the oven and let it cool for a few minutes before slicing and serving.

Nutritional Values
(per pizza, approximate)
- 240 cal
- Fat: 10g
- Carbohydrates: 32g
- Protein: 6g

SUN-DRIED TOMATO AND BASIL FOCACCIA

Dough Recipe
Classic Focaccia Dough

Ingredients
- Classic focaccia dough, ready to use
- 0.5 cup sun-dried tomatoes, chopped
- 0.25 cup fresh basil leaves, chopped
- 0.25 cup olive oil
- 1 tsp coarse salt

Preparation
1. Preheat the oven to 425°F (220°C).
2. Take the prepared Classic Focaccia Dough and transfer it to a greased baking sheet or a rectangular baking pan.
3. Gently stretch and press the dough to fit the pan, creating an even layer.
4. Sprinkle chopped sun-dried tomatoes and fresh basil leaves evenly over the dough.
5. Drizzle olive oil over the top and sprinkle coarse salt.
6. Bake in the preheated oven for about 20 to 25 minutes or until the focaccia is golden brown.
7. Remove from the oven and let it cool for a few minutes before slicing and serving.

Nutritional Values
(per pizza, approximate)
- 210 cal
- Fat: 8g
- Carbohydrates: 31g
- Protein: 5g

ROASTED VEGETABLE FOCACCIA

Dough Recipe
Classic Focaccia Dough

Ingredients
- Classic focaccia dough, ready to use
- Assorted vegetables (e.g., bell peppers, zucchini, eggplant), sliced
- 0.25 cup olive oil
- 1 tsp coarse salt
- Fresh herbs (such as thyme or rosemary), for garnish (optional)

Nutritional Values
(per pizza, approximate)
- 180 cal
- Fat: 7g
- Carbohydrates: 25g
- Protein: 4g

Preparation
1. Preheat the oven to 425°F (220°C).
2. Take the prepared Classic Focaccia Dough and transfer it to a greased baking sheet or a rectangular baking pan.
3. Gently stretch and press the dough to fit the pan, creating an even layer.
4. Arrange the sliced vegetables evenly over the dough.
5. Drizzle olive oil over the top and sprinkle coarse salt.
6. Bake in the preheated oven for about 20 to 25 minutes or until the focaccia is golden brown and the vegetables are roasted.
7. Remove from the oven and garnish with fresh herbs, if desired.
8. Let it cool for a few minutes before slicing and serving.

GRILLED CHICKEN AND PESTO FOCACCIA

Dough Recipe
Classic Focaccia Dough

Ingredients
- Classic focaccia dough, ready to use
- Grilled chicken breast slices
- Basil pesto
- 0.25 cup grated Parmesan cheese
- 0.25 cup olive oil
- 1 tsp coarse salt

Preparation
1. Preheat the oven to 425°F (220°C).
2. Take the prepared Classic Focaccia Dough and transfer it to a greased baking sheet or a rectangular baking pan.
3. Gently stretch and press the dough to fit the pan, creating an even layer.
4. Place grilled chicken breast slices evenly over the dough.
5. Spread a generous amount of basil pesto over the chicken.
6. Sprinkle grated Parmesan cheese, drizzle olive oil, and sprinkle coarse salt.
7. Bake in the preheated oven for about 20 to 25 minutes or until the focaccia is golden brown and the cheese is melted.
8. Remove from the oven and let it cool for a few minutes before slicing and serving.

Nutritional Values
(per pizza, approximate)
- 250 cal
- Fat: 11g
- Carbohydrates: 29g
- Protein: 9g

RICOTTA AND ROASTED GARLIC FOCACCIA

Dough Recipe
Classic Focaccia Dough

Ingredients
- Classic focaccia dough, ready to use
- 0.5 cup ricotta cheese
- Roasted garlic cloves
- 0.25 cup olive oil
- 1 tsp coarse salt

Preparation
1. Preheat the oven to 425°F (220°C).
2. Take the prepared Classic Focaccia Dough and transfer it to a greased baking sheet or a rectangular baking pan.
3. Gently stretch and press the dough to fit the pan, creating an even layer.
4. Spread ricotta cheese evenly over the dough.
5. Place roasted garlic cloves on top of the ricotta.
6. Drizzle olive oil and sprinkle coarse salt.
7. Bake in the preheated oven for about 20 to 25 minutes or until the focaccia is golden brown.
8. Remove from the oven and let it cool for a few minutes before slicing and serving.

Nutritional Values
(per pizza, approximate)
- 230 cal
- Fat: 10g
- Carbohydrates: 29g
- Protein: 7g

GOAT CHEESE AND CARAMELIZED ONION FOCACCIA

Dough Recipe
Classic Focaccia Dough

Ingredients
- Classic focaccia dough, ready to use
- Goat cheese, crumbled
- Caramelized onions
- 0.25 cup olive oil
- 1 tsp coarse salt

Preparation
1. Preheat the oven to 425°F (220°C).
2. Take the prepared Classic Focaccia Dough and transfer it to a greased baking sheet or a rectangular baking pan.
3. Gently stretch and press the dough to fit the pan, creating an even layer.
4. Sprinkle crumbled goat cheese evenly over the dough.
5. Spread caramelized onions on top of the cheese.
6. Drizzle olive oil and sprinkle coarse salt.
7. Bake in the preheated oven for about 20 to 25 minutes or until the focaccia golden brown and the cheese is slightly melted.
8. Remove from the oven and let it cool for a few minutes before slicing and serving.

Nutritional Values
(per pizza, approximate)
- 240 cal
- Fat: 11g
- Carbohydrates: 30g
- Protein: 6g

SMOKED SALMON AND DILL FOCACCIA

Dough Recipe
Classic Focaccia Dough

Ingredients
- Classic focaccia dough, ready to use
- Thinly-sliced smoked salmon
- Fresh dill sprigs
- 0.25 cup olive oil
- 1 tsp coarse salt

Preparation
1. Preheat the oven to 425°F (220°C).
2. Take the prepared Classic Focaccia Dough and transfer it to a greased baking sheet or a rectangular baking pan.
3. Gently stretch and press the dough to fit the pan, creating an even layer.
4. Arrange the thinly sliced smoked salmon evenly over the dough.
5. Place fresh dill sprigs on top of the salmon.
6. Drizzle olive oil and sprinkle coarse salt.
7. Bake in the preheated oven for about 20 to 25 minutes or until the focaccia is golden brown.
8. Remove from the oven and let it cool for a few minutes before slicing and serving.

Nutritional Values
(per pizza, approximate)
- 220 cal
- Fat: 10g
- Carbohydrates: 28g
- Protein: 9g

BALSAMIC GLAZED PEAR AND GORGONZOLA

Dough Recipe
Classic Focaccia Dough

Ingredients
- Classic focaccia dough, ready to use
- Ripe pears, sliced
- Balsamic glaze
- Crumbled Gorgonzola cheese
- 0.25 cup olive oil
- 1 tsp coarse salt

Preparation
1. Preheat the oven to 425°F (220°C).
2. Take the prepared Classic Focaccia Dough and transfer it to a greased baking sheet or a rectangular baking pan.
3. Gently stretch and press the dough to fit the pan, creating an even layer.
4. Arrange the sliced pears evenly over the dough.
5. Drizzle balsamic glaze over the pears.
6. Sprinkle crumbled Gorgonzola cheese on top.
7. Drizzle olive oil and sprinkle coarse salt.
8. Bake in the preheated oven for about 20 to 25 minutes or until the focaccia is golden brown and the cheese is melted.
9. Remove from the oven and let it cool for a few minutes before slicing and serving.

Nutritional Values
(per pizza, approximate)
- 260 cal
- Fat: 12g
- Carbohydrates: 32g
- Protein: 6g

DESSERT, SWEET AND FRUITY PIZZAS

In Italy, traditional pizza is primarily savory, but abroad it's common to find sweet and creative pizzas. Sweet pizza is an original variation that combines the love for pizza with the irresistible sweetness of desserts. Typically, the base of sweet pizza is similar to its savory counterpart, but it's enriched with sweet ingredients like chocolate, caramel, fresh fruit, jams, and creams before being baked.

Sweet pizzas can be served as a dessert after a meal or even as a delightful alternative to traditional sweets. Some famous variations include pizza with Nutella and strawberries, pizza with pastry cream and fresh fruit, or pizza with dark chocolate and marshmallows. These sweet versions of pizza offer an explosion of flavors and an intriguing mix of the crispness of the crust and the sweetness of the ingredients.

If you're a fan of desserts and unusual flavors, sweet pizza might be a taste experience worth trying at least once!

NUTELLA AND STRAWBERRY PIZZA

Dough Recipe
New York-Style

Ingredients
- Pizza dough (New York-style), ready to use
- 2 tbsp Nutella
- 6 to 8 strawberries, sliced

Nutritional Values
(per pizza, approximate)
- 800 cal
- Fat: 24g
- Carbohydrates: 128g
- Protein: 12g

Preparation
1. Preheat the oven to 425°F (220°C) and prepare a baking sheet by lining it with parchment paper.
2. Take the ball of pizza dough and roll it out on the baking sheet, shaping it into a round or rectangular shape according to your preference.
3. Spread the 2 tablespoons of Nutella evenly over the sweet pizza dough base.
4. Arrange the sliced strawberries on top of the Nutella, covering the entire surface.
5. Place the sweet pizza in the preheated oven and bake for approximately 12 to 15 minutes, or until the dough becomes golden and crispy.
6. Remove the pizza from the oven and let it cool slightly before cutting it into slices.
7. Serve the warm Nutella and strawberry pizza and enjoy this delicious combination of chocolate and fresh fruit.

FRIED NUTELLA BANANA PIZZA

Dough Recipe
Classic Neapolitan-Style

Ingredients
- Pizza dough (Neapolitan-style), ready to use
- Nutella or chocolate-hazelnut spread
- Sliced bananas
- Powdered sugar
- Vegetable oil for frying

Nutritional Values
(per pizza, approximate)
- 880 cal
- Fat: 35g
- Carbohydrates: 130g
- Protein: 15g

Preparation
1. Prepare the Classic Neapolitan Dough according to the base recipe.
2. Take a dough ball and flatten it with your hands, forming a disk about 4 to 6 inches in diameter.
3. Spread a generous amount of Nutella or chocolate-hazelnut spread on the dough, leaving a border around the edges.
4. Arrange slices of bananas on top of the spread.
5. Fold the other half of the dough over the toppings and seal the edges tightly.
6. Heat vegetable oil in a deep fryer or a large pan to about 375°F (190°C).
7. Carefully place the folded pizza into the hot oil and fry until golden brown on both sides.
8. Remove the fried pizza from the oil and let it drain on paper towels.
9. Sprinkle powdered sugar over the fried pizza.
10. Serve the fried Nutella banana pizza hot and enjoy!

PASTRY CREAM AND FRESH FRUIT PIZZA

Dough Recipe
New York-Style

Ingredients
- Pizza dough (New York-style), ready to use
- Pastry cream
- Fresh fruits (strawberries, kiwi, bananas, blueberries)

Nutritional Values
(per pizza, approximate)
- 900 cal
- Fat: 30g
- Carbohydrates: 140g
- Protein: 10g

Preparation
1. Preheat the oven to 425°F (220°C) and prepare a baking sheet by lining it with parchment paper.
2. Take the ball of pizza dough and roll it out on the baking sheet, shaping it into a round or rectangular shape according to your preference.
3. Spread a generous amount of pastry cream evenly over the sweet pizza dough base.
4. Arrange sliced fresh fruits on top of the pastry cream, covering the entire surface.
5. Place the sweet pizza in the preheated oven and bake for approximately 12 to 15 minutes, or until the dough becomes golden and crispy.
6. Remove the pizza from the oven and let it cool slightly before cutting it into slices.
7. Serve the Pastry Cream and Fresh Fruit Pizza and enjoy the delightful combination of sweetness and freshness.

CHOCOLATE FONDANT AND MARSHMALLOW PIZZA

Dough Recipe
New York-Style

Ingredients
- Pizza dough (New York-style), ready to use
- Dark chocolate, melted
- Marshmallows

Nutritional Values
(per pizza, approximate)
- 950 cal
- Fat: 35g
- Carbohydrates: 150g
- Protein: 10g

Preparation
1. Preheat the oven to 425°F (220°C) and prepare a baking sheet by lining it with parchment paper.
2. Take the ball of pizza dough and roll it out on the baking sheet, shaping it into a round or rectangular shape according to your preference.
3. Spread a generous amount of melted dark chocolate evenly over the sweet pizza dough base.
4. Scatter marshmallows on top of the chocolate, covering the entire surface.
5. Place the sweet pizza in the preheated oven and bake for approximately 12 to 15 minutes, or until the dough becomes golden and crispy, and the marshmallows are slightly toasted.
6. Remove the pizza from the oven and let it cool slightly before cutting it into slices.
7. Serve the Chocolate Fondant and Marshmallow Pizza and enjoy the irresistible combination of rich chocolate and fluffy marshmallows.

HAZELNUT CREAM AND BANANA PIZZA

Dough Recipe
New York-Style

Ingredients
- Pizza dough (New York-style), ready to use
- Hazelnut cream (such as Nutella)
- Sliced bananas

Nutritional Values
(per pizza, approximate)
- 880 cal
- Fat: 25g
- Carbohydrates: 140g
- Protein: 10g

Preparation
1. Preheat the oven to 425°F (220°C) and prepare a baking sheet by lining it with parchment paper.
2. Take the ball of pizza dough and roll it out on the baking sheet, shaping it into a round or rectangular shape according to your preference.
3. Spread a generous amount of hazelnut cream evenly over the sweet pizza dough base.
4. Arrange sliced bananas on top of the hazelnut cream, covering the entire surface.
5. Place the sweet pizza in the preheated oven and bake for approximately 12 to 15 minutes, or until the dough becomes golden and crispy.
6. Remove the pizza from the oven and let it cool slightly before cutting it into slices.
7. Serve the Hazelnut Cream and Banana Pizza and indulge in the creamy and fruity delight.

STRAWBERRY JAM AND WHIPPED CREAM PIZZA

Dough Recipe
New York-Style

Ingredients
- Pizza dough (New York-style), ready to use
- Strawberry jam
- Whipped cream

Nutritional Values
(per pizza, approximate)
- 820 cal
- Fat: 20g
- Carbohydrates: 140g
- Protein: 8g

Preparation
1. Preheat the oven to 425°F (220°C) and prepare a baking sheet by lining it with parchment paper.
2. Take the ball of pizza dough and roll it out on the baking sheet, shaping it into a round or rectangular shape according to your preference.
3. Spread a layer of strawberry jam evenly over the sweet pizza dough base.
4. Dollop generous amounts of whipped cream on top of the strawberry jam,
5. Place the sweet pizza in the preheated oven and bake for approximately 12 to 15 minutes, or until the dough becomes golden and crispy.
6. Remove the pizza from the oven and let it cool slightly before cutting it into slices.
7. Serve the Strawberry Jam and Whipped Cream Pizza and enjoy the delightful combination of sweet jam and fluffy cream.

CARAMELIZED APPLE AND CINNAMON PIZZA

Dough Recipe
New York-Style

Ingredients
- Pizza dough (New York-style), ready to use
- Sliced and caramelized apples
- Ground cinnamon

Nutritional Values
(per pizza, approximate)
- 900 cal
- Fat: 25g
- Carbohydrates: 140g
- Protein: 8g

Preparation
1. Preheat the oven to 425°F (220°C) and prepare a baking sheet by lining it with parchment paper.
2. Take the ball of pizza dough and roll it out on the baking sheet, shaping it into a round or rectangular shape according to your preference.
3. Spread a layer of sliced and caramelized apples evenly over the sweet pizza dough base.
4. Sprinkle ground cinnamon generously over the apples, covering the entire surface.
5. Place the sweet pizza in the preheated oven and bake for approximately 12 to 15 minutes, or until the dough becomes golden and crispy.
6. Remove the pizza from the oven and let it cool slightly before cutting it into slices.
7. Serve the Caramelized Apple and Cinnamon Pizza and savor the flavors of autumn with warm and spiced notes.

RICOTTA, HONEY, AND WALNUT PIZZA

Dough Recipe
New York-Style

Ingredients
- Pizza dough (New York-style), ready to use
- Fresh ricotta cheese
- Honey
- Chopped walnuts

Nutritional Values
(per pizza, approximate)
- 850 cal
- Fat: 20g
- Carbohydrates: 140g
- Protein: 10g

Preparation
1. Preheat the oven to 425°F (220°C) and prepare a baking sheet by lining it with parchment paper.
2. Take the ball of pizza dough and roll it out on the baking sheet, shaping it into a round or rectangular shape according to your preference.
3. Spread a layer of fresh ricotta cheese evenly over the sweet pizza dough base.
4. Drizzle honey generously over the ricotta cheese and sprinkle chopped walnuts on top, covering the entire surface.
5. Place the sweet pizza in the preheated oven and bake for approximately 12 to 15 minutes, or until the dough becomes golden and crispy.
6. Remove the pizza from the oven and let it cool slightly before cutting it into slices.
7. Serve the Ricotta, Honey, and Walnut Pizza and enjoy the combination of creamy sweetness and crunchy walnuts.

PISTACHIO CREAM AND WHITE CHOCOLATE PIZZA

Dough Recipe
New York-Style

Ingredients
- Pizza dough (New York-style), ready to use
- Pistachio cream
- White chocolate shavings

Nutritional Values
(per pizza, approximate)
- 850 cal
- Fat: 20g
- Carbohydrates: 140g
- Protein: 8g

Preparation
1. Preheat the oven to 425°F (220°C) and prepare a baking sheet by lining it with parchment paper.
2. Take the ball of pizza dough and roll it out on the baking sheet, shaping it into a round or rectangular shape according to your preference.
3. Spread a layer of pistachio cream evenly over the sweet pizza dough base.
4. Sprinkle white chocolate shavings generously over the pistachio cream, covering the entire surface.
5. Place the sweet pizza in the preheated oven and bake for approximately 12 to 15 minutes, or until the dough becomes golden and crispy.
6. Remove the pizza from the oven and let it cool slightly before cutting it into slices.
7. Serve the Pistachio Cream and White Chocolate Pizza and enjoy the harmonious blend of creamy flavors and subtly sweet notes.

VANILLA CREAM AND MIXED BERRY PIZZA

Dough Recipe
New York-Style

Ingredients
- Pizza dough (New York-style), ready to use
- Vanilla cream
- Mixed berries (such as strawberries, raspberries, blueberries, and blackberries)

Nutritional Values
(per pizza, approximate)
- 800 cal
- Fat: 15g
- Carbohydrates: 150g
- Protein: 10g

Preparation
1. Preheat the oven to 425°F (220°C) and line a baking sheet with parchment paper.
2. Take the ball of pizza dough and roll it out on the prepared baking sheet, shaping it into a round or rectangular shape according to your preference.
3. Spread a layer of vanilla cream evenly over the sweet pizza dough base, covering the entire surface.
4. Arrange the mixed berries on top of the vanilla cream, distributing them evenly across the pizza.
5. Place the pizza in the preheated oven and bake for approximately 12 to 15 minutes, or until the dough becomes golden and slightly crispy.
6. Remove the pizza from the oven and allow it to cool slightly before cutting it into slices.
7. Serve the Vanilla Cream and Mixed Berry Pizza and savor the delightful combination of creamy flavors and the natural sweetness of the mixed berries.

PINEAPPLE AND COCONUT PIZZA

Dough Recipe
New York-Style

Ingredients

- Pizza dough (New York-style), ready to use
- Sliced pineapple
- Toasted coconut flakes

Nutritional Values
(per pizza, approximate)

- 820 cal
- Fat: 20g
- Carbohydrates: 140g
- Protein: 8g

Preparation

1. Preheat the oven to 425°F (220°C) and prepare a baking sheet by lining it with parchment paper.
2. Take the ball of pizza dough and roll it out on the baking sheet, shaping it into a round or rectangular shape according to your preference.
3. Arrange sliced pineapple on top of the sweet pizza dough, covering the entire surface.
4. Sprinkle toasted coconut flakes generously over the pineapple, ensuring even coverage
5. Place the sweet pizza in the preheated oven and bake for approximately 12 to 15 minutes, or until the dough becomes golden and crispy.
6. Remove the pizza from the oven and let it cool slightly before cutting it into slices.
7. Serve the Pineapple and Coconut Pizza for a tropical twist on a sweet pizza experience.

CONCLUSION

Thank you for joining me on this incredibly tasty adventure in the world of pizza. Throughout these pages, I've tried to convey a bit of the Italian atmosphere that is deeply ingrained in my family's history and, of course, in the origins of this extraordinary food that the entire world goes crazy for.

I wanted homemade good pizza to be accessible to everyone, not just a select few, that's why I've done my best to simplify certain steps without delving too much into technicalities. However, if after your initial kitchen experiments, you feel a calling to dive even deeper, know that the world of leavened dough, flours, and dough hydration combinations is truly vast, and there's plenty of room for exploration for you.

Personally, what I love is providing practical tools and information to anyone who wants to experience the joy of making their first successful pizzas. Starting from the basics, you have now learned about the essential tools and ingredients needed to create the perfect pizza dough. Whether you prefer the classic Neapolitan-style, the thin crust of New York-style, or the deliciousness of Chicago's deep-dish pizza, you have a variety of dough recipes to choose from to **surprise yourself and never get bored over 1,000 days and beyond of pizza enjoyment.**

I'm certain I've also caught your attention with focaccia and fried pizza, and undoubtedly, you're ready to delight your guests with sweet pizza recipes as well.

With this comprehensive collection of recipes, techniques, and tips, you're now prepared to unleash your creativity in the kitchen and impress family and friends with your homemade pizzas. Remember, in the kitchen, the joy lies not only in the final result but also in the process of creating and sharing a meal prepared with love. After all, I believe that's the secret ingredient of my Aunt Rosaria's pizza.

So, grab your apron, preheat the oven, and let the aroma of freshly-baked pizza fill your home. Enjoy the journey and savor every bite of your homemade pizza creations.

Buon appetito!

CONVERSION CHART

Oven Temperatures

NO FAN	FAN FORCED	FARENHEIT
120 °C	100 °C	250 °C
150 °C	130 °C	300 °C
160 °C	140 °C	325 °C
180 °C	160 °C	350°C
190 °C	170 °C	375°C
200 °C	180 °C	400°C
230 °C	210 °C	450°C
250 °C	230 °C	500°C

Sr Flour   =   Self Raising

Cup and Spoons

CUP	METRIC
1/4 cup	60 ml
1/3 cup	80 ml
1/2 cup	125ml
1 cup	250 ml
SPOONS	**SPOONS**
1/4 teaspoon	1.25 ml
1/2 teaspoon	2.5 ml
1 teaspoon	5 ml
2 teaspoon	10 ml
1 Tablespoon	20 ml

Liquids

Cup	Metric	Imperial
	30ml	1 fl oz
1/4 Cup	60ml	2 fl oz
1/3 Cup	80 ml	31/2 fl oz
	100 ml	23/4 fl oz
1/2 Cup	125 ml	4 fl oz
	150 ml	5 fl oz
3/4 Cup	180 ml	6 fl oz
	200 ml	7 fl oz
1 Cup	250 ml	83/4 fl oz
11/4 Cups	310 ml	101/2 fl oz
11/2 Cups	375 ml	13 fl oz
13/4 Cups	430 ml	15 fl oz
	475 ml	16 fl oz
2 Cups	500 ml	17 fl oz
21/2 Cups	625 ml	211/2 fl oz
3 Cups	750 ml	26 fl oz
4 Cups	1L	35 fl oz
5 Cups	1.25L	44 fl oz
6 Cups	1.5L	52 fl oz
8 Cups	2L	70 fl oz
10 Cups	2.5L	88 fl oz

Mass

Imperial	Metric
1/4 oz	10g
1/2 oz	15 g
1 oz	30 g
2 oz	60 g
3 oz	90 g
4 oz (1/4 lb)	125 g
5 oz	155 g
6 oz	185 g
7 oz	220 g
8 oz (1/2 lb)	250 g
9 oz	280 g
10 oz	315 g
11 oz	345 g
12 oz (3/4 lb)	375 g
13 oz	410 g
14 oz	440 g
15 oz	470 g
16 oz (1 lb)	500 g
24 oz (11/2 lb)	750 g
32 oz (2 lb)	1kg
48 oz (3 lb)	1.5kg

ALPHABETICAL INGREDIENTS INDEX

Enhance your reading experience with the

FULL VIDEO TUTORIAL

FULL VIDEO TUTORIAL

How to make the perfect
Classic Neapolitan Pizza

SCAN ME or

https://bit.ly/pizzavideotutorial

LEAVE A SUPER QUICK REVIEW ON AMAZON.COM

MY PIZZA RECIPES

Pizza Name _____

Dough Recipe _____

Dough Notes _____

_____

_____

Preparation _____

_____

_____

_____

_____

_____

Ingredients

_____

_____

_____

_____

_____

_____

_____

Oven Temperature _____

Cooking Time _____

Pizza Name _____

Dough Recipe _____

Dough Notes _____

_____

_____

Preparation _____

_____

_____

_____

_____

Ingredients

_____

_____

_____

_____

_____

_____

_____

Oven Temperature _____

Cooking Time _____

MY PIZZA RECIPES

Pizza Name _____

Dough Recipe _____

Dough Notes _____

_____

_____

Preparation _____

_____

_____

_____

_____

_____

Ingredients

_____

_____

_____

_____

_____

_____

_____

_____

_____

Oven Temperature _____

Cooking Time _____

Pizza Name _____

Dough Recipe _____

Dough Notes _____

_____

_____

Preparation _____

_____

_____

_____

_____

Ingredients

_____

_____

_____

_____

_____

_____

_____

_____

Oven Temperature _____

Cooking Time _____

MY PIZZA RECIPES

Pizza Name _____

Dough Recipe _____

Dough Notes _____

_____

Preparation _____

_____

_____

_____

_____

_____

Ingredients

_____

_____

_____

_____

_____

_____

_____

_____

Oven Temperature _____

Cooking Time _____

Pizza Name _____

Dough Recipe _____

Dough Notes _____

_____

_____

Preparation _____

_____

_____

_____

_____

Ingredients

_____

_____

_____

_____

_____

_____

_____

Oven Temperature _____

Cooking Time _____

ac7b7e25-b69c-45ee-b6f8-bae29f2df48fR01